DR. MOHAMED-ALI IBRAHIM

Mastering Data Quality Evaluation

ISO 19157:2023

Practical Implementation in Geospatial Data Management

Mastering Data Quality Evaluation ISO 19157:2023

Practical Implementation in Geospatial Data Management

Dr. Mohamed-Ali Ibrahim

DEDICATION

This book is dedicated to all the professionals and organizations working tirelessly to ensure the highest standards of data quality. Your commitment to precision, consistency, and integrity shapes the future of geospatial data and drives informed decision-making across industries.

May this work inspire further advancements in data governance and quality evaluation

Introduction

In an increasingly data-driven world, the quality of geospatial data is paramount. **ISO 19157:2023** provides a comprehensive framework for evaluating and ensuring the quality of geographic information, ensuring that the data you rely on for decision-making is accurate, consistent, and trustworthy.

This book, *Mastering Data Quality Evaluation: ISO 19157:2023*, is designed to help you apply the principles and requirements of the standard to real-world geospatial data management. By focusing on practical steps and clear explanations, this guide will empower you to confidently evaluate and report the quality of your data, whether you are handling large datasets, managing data governance initiatives, or preparing for audits and compliance.

Benefits

- **Improved Data Quality**: Learn how to assess, evaluate, and enhance the quality of your geospatial data in alignment with the internationally recognized **ISO 19157:2023** standard.
- **Practical, Actionable Insights**: The book offers easy-to-follow steps on how to implement data quality evaluation techniques without delving into overly technical or complex details.
- **Clear Reporting**: Master the art of documenting your findings in clear, traceable reports, which will support your data governance initiatives and ensure compliance.
- **Optimized Sampling and Evaluation**: Understand the importance of sampling and how to implement it effectively for accurate results, ensuring representativeness and repeatability in your data quality evaluations.
- **Compliance with Global Standards**: Gain insight into maintaining conformance with ISO 19157 and how this can help your organization meet international quality standards, improve data interoperability, and boost stakeholder trust.

Who is it for?

This book is perfect for anyone involved in geospatial data management, including:

- **Geospatial Data Professionals**: GIS specialists, data analysts, and data scientists looking to deepen their understanding of data quality standards and improve their evaluation practices.
- **Quality Managers**: Professionals responsible for ensuring that data meets specific standards and quality criteria.
- **Decision-Makers**: Managers and executives involved in overseeing data governance, ensuring that high-quality, reliable data is used for business decisions.
- **Compliance Officers**: Those tasked with ensuring data meets regulatory and international standards, including ISO conformance.

Why Choose This Book?

- **Comprehensive Yet Accessible**: This book distills the principles of ISO 19157:2023 into practical, actionable guidance, allowing you to apply it effectively without the need for deep technical expertise.
- **Focus on Real-World Applications**: The content is designed for easy integration into your daily workflows, with practical examples and step-by-step instructions on implementing ISO-compliant data quality evaluation processes.
- **Clear and Concise**: It avoids jargon-heavy explanations and delivers the key takeaways in a straightforward, understandable manner, making complex standards accessible to all.
- **Stay Ahead of Trends**: By choosing this book, you are staying ahead in the ever-evolving landscape of geospatial data, ensuring your practices remain aligned with the latest international data quality standards.

DR. MOHAMED-ALI IBRAHIM

Dr. Mohamed-Ali Ibrahim is a renowned expert in data quality management, with over 25 years of experience in market expansion, operational excellence, and business innovation. As the founder of **IQC-Vienna**, he works with organizations to enhance their data quality systems, ensuring sustainable growth and improved decision-making. His expertise in data quality evaluation has helped numerous businesses achieve operational efficiency and better align their processes with international standards.

Visionary Leader in Quality Management and International Standards

He is the author of over 80 professional publications in English, Arabic, and German—focusing on business administration, quality and risk management, and translation studies. His latest work is *"**Mastering Advance Value Engineering**."*

As an MBA lecturer, expert in digital transformation, and Senior Lead Auditor, Dr. Ibrahim specializes in international future standards, including **ISO 19157:2023**, **ISO 9001, ISO 22301, ISO 45001, ISO 27001, ISO 14001, ISO 18587, and ISO 20771.**

He is recognized as a dedicated advocate of institutional quality and is committed to building resilient, future-proof organizational structures.

His expertise is valued across industries. His clients include ministries, government agencies, public figures, and leading organizations from a wide range of sectors.

With a unique combination of academic depth and practical implementation expertise, Dr. Ibrahim is considered a beacon of excellence in promoting high-

Certifications: Certified Lead Auditor for Key ISO Standards

quality standards and innovative practical solutions. His significant contributions to quality management and international standardization have also made him a sought-after strategic advISOr.

ISO Standard	Area of Specialization
ISO 19157:2023	Geospatial Data Evaluation
ISO 22301	Business Continuity Management
ISO 9001	Quality Management Systems
ISO 45001	Occupational Health and Safety Management Systems
ISO 14001	Environmental Management Systems
ISO 18587	Machine Translation Post-Editing
ISO 20228	Interpreter Services - Legal Interpreting
ISO 13611	Community Interpreting
ISO 18841	Interpreter Services
ISO 21001	Educational Management Systems
ISO 17100	Translation Service Providers
ISO 21998	Healthcare Interpreting
ISO 23155	Conference Interpreting
ISO 20771	Legal Translation
ISO 27001	Information Security Management Systems

Practical Experience in the Kingdom of Saudi Arabia

Dr. Ibrahim has advised leading Saudi institutions—including the Ministry of Culture, Royal Court, and SIDF—on quality management and ISO certifications, notably ISO 17100 and ISO 9001. He helped establish high-performing translation and communication units.

Region/Institution	Activity/Role
Kingdom of Saudi Arabia	Strategic consulting and leading workshops in **Quality Management** for high-ranking government institutions (e.g., **Ministry of Culture, Royal Court, SIDF**)
ISO Certifications	Led the introduction and implementation of **ISO 17100** (Translation Services) and **ISO 9001** (Quality Management)

International	Engaged in consulting and training in **Austria**, **USA**, **UK**, **Egypt**, **UAE**, **Saudi Arabia**, **Algeria**, **Jordan**

Lectures & Teaching

Since 1998, Dr. Mohamed-Ali Ibrahim has been a keynote speaker and lecturer, sharing expertise in quality management, translation studies, and risk management at international conferences and Vienna University of Applied Sciences.

Awards:

- **Top Expert 2025** – *ERFOLG-Magazine* (Quality & Risk Management)
- **Austrian State Award** – Business growth & excellence
- **Recognized** in German & British award programs
- **Expert of the Year (2021–2024)** – Innovation & client focus
- **Reviewer** – Saudi Center for Accreditation
- **EFQM Assessor** – European Foundation for Quality Management
- **Winner** – International German Prize, Best Practice Award Austria, SABRE Award (UK)

Publications

Dr. Mohamed-Ali Ibrahim has authored over **80+ books** on **Amazon**. These publications cover topics in **business management**, **quality management**, and **real estate management**.

Explore Dr. Ibrahim's Books on Amazon

(https://www.amazon.com/stores/author/B09YXDBTV5)

Academy IQC Vienna

Mastering Data Quality Evaluation: ISO 19157:2023

Welcome to Academy IQC Vienna — your hub for innovative online learning and resources to boost quality management, ISO 9001:2015 compliance, and business performance through tailored courses, e-forms, and coaching.

Service	Description	Link
E-Workshop	Join interactive e-workshops that provide in-depth training on **ISO standards**, **quality management**, and **risk management**. Engage in practical exercises.	https://academy.iqc-vienna.com/e-workshop/
E-Coaching	Get personalized coaching from industry experts. Whether you need guidance on **ISO certification**, **audit preparation**, or process optimization.	https://academy.iqc-vienna.com/e-coaching/
Online Courses	Take advantage of our self-paced online courses designed to help you master **ISO standards**, enhance **quality management**, and develop necessary skills.	https://academy.iqc-vienna.com/online-courses/
Documentation Kits	Streamline your **ISO 9001** implementation with comprehensive documentation kits, including templates for **policies**, **procedures**, and **forms**.	https://academy.iqc-vienna.com/documentation-kits/

Table of Contents

CHAPTER 1

Introduction to ISO 19157:2023

PURPOSE OF THE STANDARD

ISO 19157:2023 defines the principles and guidelines for evaluating the **quality of geographic data**. The standard provides a **structured framework** that helps organizations measure, assess, and improve the quality of their **geospatial data** to meet **international standards** and support decision-making.

The purpose of this standard is not just to provide definitions of data quality but to **establish a universal method** that ensures geographic information is both **reliable** and **usable**. With data being the backbone of numerous **business operations**, **government initiatives**, and **scientific research**, ensuring its accuracy and reliability is critical.

OVERVIEW OF ISO 19157:2023

ISO 19157:2023 is the international standard for **geospatial data quality evaluation**. It includes general requirements for evaluating **data quality** and provides a **comprehensive model** for expressing data quality. The standard includes:

- **Data quality elements**: These are the core aspects such as **completeness**, **consistency**, **accuracy**, **usability**, and others that define the quality of geographic information.
- **Evaluation methods**: The standard outlines how data quality should be evaluated using **measurable indicators** and **evaluation frameworks**.
- **Reporting standards**: Clear guidelines on how to document and report data quality, ensuring transparency and traceability.

The standard is essential for organizations looking to align their **data management practices** with **global benchmarks** while maintaining flexibility for **domain-specific needs**.

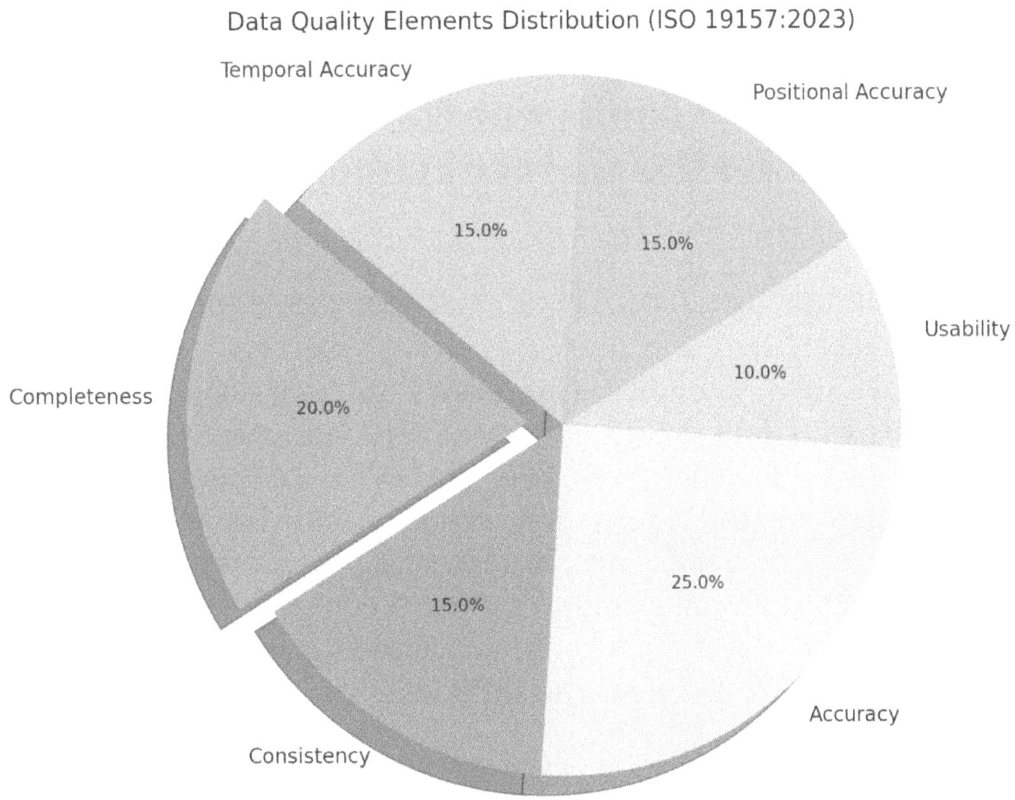

IMPORTANCE OF DATA QUALITY IN GEOSPATIAL INFORMATION

The **quality of geospatial data** directly impacts the **effectiveness** and **accuracy** of decisions made using that data. Whether it's for **urban planning**, **disaster management**, or **environmental monitoring**, **poor quality data** can lead to incorrect conclusions, inefficient operations, and costly mistakes.

Ensuring **high data quality** is essential in:

- **Decision-Making**: Accurate and reliable data supports informed decision-making, ensuring that actions taken are based on factual, well-evaluated information.

- **Interoperability**: In the global context, geospatial data often needs to be shared across different systems and organizations. **Standardized data quality** ensures **interoperability** and reduces **data integration issues**.
- **Trust and Accountability**: Quality data builds **trust** between stakeholders, ensuring that decisions made from data are **transparent** and **auditable**.

How ISO 19157:2023 Aligns with National And Organizational Data Governance Frameworks (E.G., Saudi Vision 2030)

1. STANDARDIZING DATA QUALITY ACROSS GOVERNMENT ENTITIES

ISO 19157:2023 offers a **unified framework** for evaluating and ensuring the **quality of geospatial data** across all sectors. This alignment with Saudi Arabia's **Vision 2030** allows different government entities to implement a **standardized approach** to **data quality evaluation**, ensuring **consistency**, **reliability**, and **interoperability** of geographic data across multiple platforms. The standard's **universal approach** is pivotal in improving data **accuracy** and **efficiency**, which is key to achieving the Kingdom's goals of enhancing government transparency, service delivery, and overall **operational efficiency**.

2. ENHANCING DATA GOVERNANCE AND COMPLIANCE

ISO 19157:2023 plays a critical role in supporting **national data governance regulations** such as those outlined by the **National Data Management Office (NDMO)** and **SDAIA**. By providing clear guidelines for **data evaluation** and **quality reporting**, the standard helps Saudi Arabia's government meet the regulatory requirements for data **transparency**, **security**, and **interoperability**. This directly supports the objectives of the **National Data Governance Interim Regulation**, which emphasizes the need for clear **data classification**, effective **data sharing**, and the protection of **citizen data**. ISO 19157:2023's ability to assess **data quality** aligns perfectly with these goals, ensuring that the Kingdom's data ecosystem operates in **compliance** with both national and international standards.

3. SUPPORTING OPEN DATA INITIATIVES

Saudi Arabia's **open data platform** (open.data.gov.sa) plays a key role in fostering **public trust** and **innovation** through transparency. By adhering to the **ISO 19157:2023** standard, government datasets on this platform can be **evaluated** for **quality**, ensuring that the public and external partners can confidently utilize these datasets for research, innovation, and application development. The standard's emphasis on clear **metadata** and **quality reporting** allows users to verify the **accuracy** and **usability** of data, further supporting **Vision 2030's** goal of building a **data-driven economy** where **transparency** and **collaboration** thrive.

4. ENABLING DATA-DRIVEN DECISION-MAKING

The **Vision 2030** transformation focuses on **data analytics, artificial intelligence (AI)**, and **smart decision-making** across government sectors such as **urban planning**, **healthcare**, and **infrastructure development**. Implementing ISO 19157:2023 ensures that **high-quality geospatial data** is used in these critical decision-making processes. With its guidelines for evaluating data **accuracy**, **completeness**, and **usability**, the standard enables decision-makers to use **reliable data** to create **data-driven solutions**, which directly supports the Kingdom's goals of **economic diversification** and **improved public services**.

5. FACILITATING INTERNATIONAL COLLABORATION

ISO 19157:2023 is an **internationally recognized standard**, making it a crucial element for Saudi Arabia as it strives to integrate its data governance frameworks into the **global digital economy**. The **standard's compatibility** with other international standards promotes **collaboration** and **data sharing** with other nations and international organizations. This aligns with Saudi Arabia's **Vision 2030**, which seeks to enhance the Kingdom's **global competitiveness** by **fostering international partnerships** and **collaborations** in technology, data management, and innovation.

SUMMARY

ISO 19157:2023 is central to Saudi Arabia's **data governance** strategy under **Vision 2030**. By ensuring **standardized, high-quality geospatial data** evaluation and reporting, it enables **interoperability**, supports **data-driven decision-making**, and enhances **transparency** across government sectors. Furthermore, it facilitates compliance with national regulations and encourages **international collaboration**, making it a key enabler of Saudi Arabia's **data-centric transformation**.

KEY GOALS AND RELEVANCE

WHY ISO 19157 MATTERS FOR GEOSPATIAL DATA

ISO 19157:2023 is critical for ensuring **reliable and high-quality geospatial data** in a world that increasingly relies on geographic information for **decision-making**. This standard directly addresses the challenges of managing and maintaining **accurate** and **consistent** data across diverse systems, governments, and organizations.

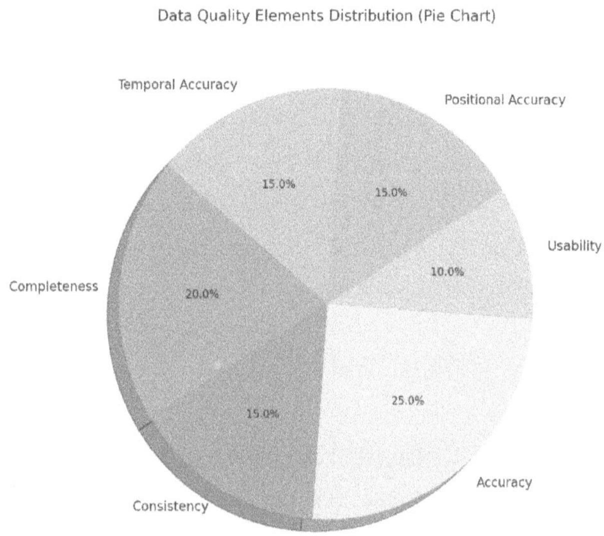

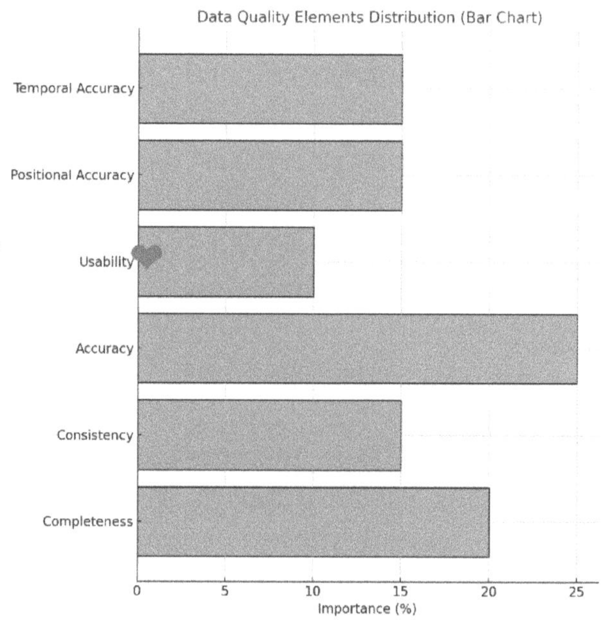

As geospatial data becomes integral to sectors like **urban planning**, **environmental monitoring**, **disaster management**, and **infrastructure development**, the demand for **trusted, quality data** has grown. ISO 19157:2023 offers the **framework** and **methodologies** required to evaluate and improve the quality of geospatial data, ensuring it meets **international standards**.

By adopting **ISO 19157**, organizations and governments can make **informed decisions** based on **trustworthy geographic data**, ultimately improving the effectiveness of their operations, policies, and services. This aligns with global initiatives, such as **Saudi Vision 2030**, where geospatial data is essential for achieving goals like **smart cities** and **data-driven governance**.

HOW ISO 19157 ENSURES ACCURATE, CONSISTENT, AND USABLE GEOGRAPHIC DATA

ISO 19157:2023 plays a fundamental role in ensuring that geospatial data is **accurate**, **consistent**, and **usable** by focusing on key principles and elements of data quality. These principles guide how data is collected, evaluated, and reported to guarantee that it meets specific quality standards:

- **Accuracy**: The standard defines methods for ensuring data **correctness** and **reliability**. By assessing **positional** and **temporal accuracy**, ISO 19157 ensures that geographic data represents the real world as closely as possible, reducing errors that could impact decision-making.
- **Consistency**: ISO 19157 helps ensure that geospatial data adheres to **internal logic** and **standardized formats**. This makes the data consistent across different datasets, reducing discrepancies when integrating multiple sources and ensuring interoperability across systems.
- **Usability**: By focusing on elements like **completeness** and **usability**, the standard ensures that geospatial data is not only accurate but also **relevant** and **fit for purpose**. This is crucial for users in industries such as urban planning, where data must be easily interpretable and actionable.

Additionally, the **reporting guidelines** in ISO 19157:2023 provide clear and **transparent methods** for documenting data quality, making it easier for stakeholders to **trust** the data. By standardizing these evaluation processes, the standard makes it easier to **compare data quality** across different datasets and projects.

In summary, ISO 19157:2023 ensures that geospatial data is of the highest quality, which is crucial for accurate analysis and informed decision-making. This helps reduce **risks**, **improves efficiency**, and **supports transparency** in a data-driven world.

APPLICATION OF ISO 19157

The Role of The Standard In Enhancing Data Quality Evaluation And Communication Across Different Sectors And Stakeholders

ISO 19157:2023 plays a critical role in enhancing the **evaluation** and **communication** of **geospatial data quality** across various sectors and stakeholders. By providing a structured approach for assessing, reporting, and improving data quality, the standard helps organizations across different industries achieve **consistent, reliable**, and **accurate data**.

1. STANDARDIZED EVALUATION METHODOLOGY

ISO 19157 provides a **unified framework** for evaluating data quality, ensuring that all stakeholders—whether in **government**, **private sector**, or **research institutions**—follow the same **criteria** and **methodology**. This standardization enables:

- **Consistency in Data Assessment**: Different stakeholders can evaluate data using the same principles, making it easier to compare data from multiple sources or across different regions.
- **Clear Evaluation Criteria**: The standard clearly defines **data quality elements** like **completeness**, **accuracy**, **consistency**, and **usability**, offering practical evaluation methods for each.

By standardizing the evaluation process, **ISO 19157** ensures that **data quality is objectively measured**, reducing subjectivity and variability in how data is assessed across various sectors.

2. IMPROVED DATA COMMUNICATION

Effective **data communication** is vital for decision-making, especially in **multistakeholder environments**. **ISO 19157** enhances communication by providing clear guidelines on how to document and report data quality findings. This allows different organizations and individuals to:

- **Understand Data Quality**: The standard promotes transparency in how data quality is evaluated, providing stakeholders with clear, easily interpretable

reports that include important details like **accuracy**, **confidence levels**, and **uncertainty**.
- **Build Trust**: Transparent and standardized reporting fosters **trust** in the data, which is essential for collaboration between organizations, governments, and other stakeholders.
- **Facilitate Data Sharing**: With standardized data quality reports, organizations can share and use data more effectively, leading to better collaboration and decision-making.

This improves the overall **communication process**, ensuring that all stakeholders have a clear understanding of the **data quality**, making them more confident in using the data for analysis, policy development, and operational decisions.

3. SUPPORTING DATA INTEGRATION AND INTEROPERABILITY

In today's world, data is often collected by different organizations, across different platforms, and in diverse formats. ISO 19157 helps to:

- **Promote Data Interoperability**: The standard's structured approach makes it easier to integrate data from different sources, ensuring that data meets the same **quality benchmarks** and is compatible with other datasets.
- **Facilitate Cross-Sector Collaboration**: Whether it's a **government department**, **private sector company**, or **academic institution**, ISO 19157's common framework for data quality ensures that data can be effectively shared and used across sectors, fostering collaboration and **collective decision-making**.

4. IMPACT ON DECISION-MAKING ACROSS SECTORS

ISO 19157 enhances **data-driven decision-making** in several key sectors:

- **Government**: For urban planning, disaster management, and public health, the standard ensures that the data used to make **policy decisions** is of high quality, reducing errors and improving outcomes.
- **Private Sector**: In industries like **real estate**, **transportation**, and **environmental management**, businesses rely on accurate and consistent

geospatial data to make **strategic decisions**. ISO 19157 provides them with the tools to ensure their data meets industry standards.

- **Research and Academia**: Researchers use high-quality data to draw conclusions, conduct experiments, and propose solutions. ISO 19157 enables **academia** to work with trustworthy, standardized datasets, ensuring that findings are based on **reliable data**.

5. SUPPORTING NATIONAL AND INTERNATIONAL INITIATIVES

ISO 19157:2023's global acceptance allows it to support national and international data governance frameworks. Whether it's a **national data management initiative** or **international collaboration**, the standard ensures that data quality is evaluated consistently, enabling:

- **Global ComparISOns**: Different nations and organizations can use the same criteria for evaluating data quality, making it easier to compare datasets across borders and regions.
- **Compliance with Global Data Standards**: The standard helps organizations comply with **international regulations** and **data-sharing agreements**, ensuring that geospatial data can be used seamlessly across international projects.

SUMMARY

In summary, **ISO 19157:2023** plays a vital role in improving the **evaluation and communication** of geospatial data quality across sectors and stakeholders. By providing a **consistent framework** for assessment, **standardized reporting methods**, and promoting **data integration**, the standard ensures that geospatial data is not only **accurate** and **reliable** but also **trusted** and **usable** by all stakeholders involved in decision-making processes.

CHAPTER 2

Core Principles of Data Quality Evaluation

UNDERSTANDING THE STANDARD'S STRUCTURE

ISO 19157:2023 is a **comprehensive** standard designed to guide organizations in evaluating the **quality of geospatial data**. Its structure is methodical and organized, ensuring a clear and **systematic approach** to data quality assessment.

The **structure** of the standard is laid out across several clauses, which define **key principles**, **guidelines**, and **methodologies** for evaluating geospatial data quality. The standard is designed for a wide range of users, including **governments**, **private organizations**, **research institutions**, and **data managers**, ensuring that the data evaluation process is **clear**, **consistent**, and **applicable** across diverse industries.

Key sections of the standard include:

- **Clause 1: Scope and Purpose** – This introduces the **objectives** of the standard and outlines its **application**.
- **Clause 2: Normative References** – Lists other standards and documents referenced by ISO 19157.
- **Clause 3: Terms and Definitions** – Provides the essential **terminology** used throughout the document, offering clarity on critical terms related to data quality evaluation.
- **Clause 4: General Principles** – Discusses the **core principles** of data quality evaluation, including **accuracy**, **consistency**, and **usability**.
- **Clause 5: Data Quality Elements** – Details the six key data quality elements, including **completeness**, **consistency**, **accuracy**, and **usability**.
- **Clause 6: Methods of Evaluation** – Explains the processes involved in evaluating geospatial data quality using standardized measures.

- **Clause 7: Reporting Data Quality Information** – Outlines how to document and communicate data quality evaluations clearly and transparently.

This **structured approach** ensures that all stakeholders can follow a **consistent method** for data evaluation and achieve **standardised results**.

THE SCOPE AND PURPOSE OF ISO 19157:2023 (CLAUSE 1)

The **scope** and **purpose** of **ISO 19157:2023** are outlined in **Clause 1**, which sets the foundation for the entire standard.

Scope:

ISO 19157:2023 provides a framework for the **evaluation of geospatial data quality**. The standard outlines the principles and **guidelines** for assessing how well geospatial data meets specified quality criteria. This includes measuring **accuracy**, **consistency**, **completeness**, **usability**, and other data quality elements relevant to geographic data.

Purpose:

The purpose of the standard is to **improve** and **standardize** the processes by which organizations assess, document, and report the quality of their geospatial data. The standard also aims to provide a clear framework that organizations can follow to ensure their geospatial data is **reliable**, **interoperable**, and **usable**. Through standardized practices, the **quality** of geospatial data can be consistently evaluated across different sectors, industries, and nations.

This enables **transparency** and **accountability**, ensuring that the data used in decision-making processes is of the **highest quality**.

OVERVIEW OF RELATED STANDARDS: ISO 19157-2 AND ISO 19157-3

ISO 19157:2023 is part of a broader series of standards under the **ISO 19157 family**, which governs the **quality of geospatial data**. The related standards, **ISO 19157-2** and **ISO 19157-3**, provide further details on specific aspects of data quality evaluation:

- **ISO 19157-2**: This part focuses on the **catalogue of quality measures** used to assess various quality elements of geospatial data. It provides **measures** and **metrics** that are used to quantify data quality, enabling consistent assessment across different datasets and systems. ISO 19157-2 details the specific techniques and tools for measuring aspects like **positional accuracy**, **thematic accuracy**, and **temporal accuracy**.

- **ISO 19157-3**: This part deals with the **conceptual schema** for geospatial data quality. It focuses on the **data models** and **schema structures** that define how data quality is represented within data systems. ISO 19157-3 ensures that geospatial data can be easily integrated and evaluated across different **information systems** using a **standardized format**.

Together with **ISO 19157:2023**, these standards provide a **comprehensive framework** for evaluating and ensuring the **quality of geospatial data** across various sectors.

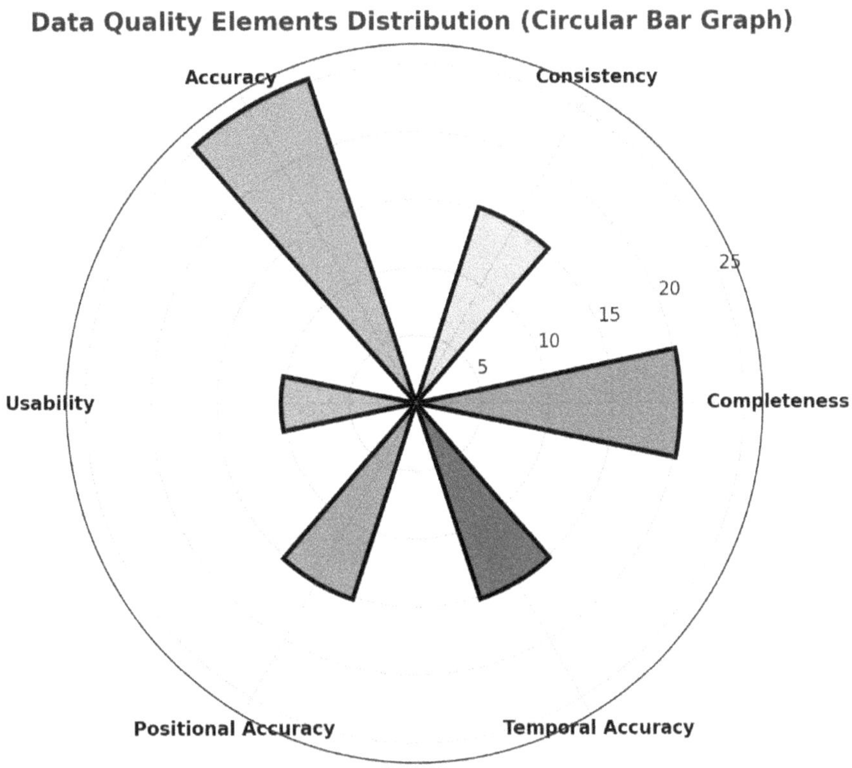

EXPLANATION OF KEY CLAUSES AND TERMINOLOGY

ISO 19157:2023 uses specific **terminology** to ensure **clarity** and **consistency** across the standard. Below is an overview of the key **clauses** and **terminology** used in the standard:

- **Data Quality Elements**: These are the core categories used to evaluate geospatial data. They include:
    - **Completeness**: The degree to which all required data is present.
    - **Consistency**: The degree to which data values adhere to predefined rules.
    - **Accuracy**: The degree to which data represents the real-world conditions accurately.
    - **Usability**: The extent to which data is fit for its intended purpose.
    - **Positional Accuracy**: The correctness of the spatial location of features.
    - **Temporal Accuracy**: The correctness of the time aspect of data.
- **Evaluation Methods**: The methods and techniques for measuring the quality of geospatial data, including direct and indirect evaluation methods, as well as how to use **sampling** and **statistical techniques** for accuracy assessment.
- **Reporting Standards**: Guidelines on how to clearly and consistently document data quality assessments. This includes reporting **metadata**, **error margins**, **uncertainty**, and any measures used to assess data quality.

SUMMARY

In this chapter, we have explored the **core structure** of ISO 19157:2023 and its related standards, including **ISO 19157-2** and **ISO 19157-3**. These standards together provide a **comprehensive framework** for evaluating, reporting, and improving the quality of geospatial data. The standard's clear methodology ensures **transparency** and **consistency** in the way data quality is assessed, making it easier for organizations across sectors to use high-quality geospatial data for decision-making.

PRINCIPLES OF DATA QUALITY (CLAUSE 4)

STANDARDIZED DATA QUALITY PRINCIPLES

ISO 19157:2023 defines core principles for evaluating geospatial data quality. These principles, standardized across sectors, ensure data meets global benchmarks for **accuracy**, **reliability**, and **usability**.

TABLE 1: Data Quality Principles Overview

Principle	Description	Importance
Consistency	Ensures data adheres to internal logic and rules, making it free from contradictions.	Helps to integrate and compare datasets across systems without discrepancies.
Comparability	Ensures data from different sources can be meaningfully compared and integrated.	Allows for seamless use and combination of data from multiple sources.
Transparency	Ensures the data quality evaluation process is open and well-documented.	Builds trust by making data quality assessments understandable and verifiable.

THE IMPORTANCE OF CONSISTENCY, COMPARABILITY, AND TRANSPARENCY

Below is a deeper look into the importance of each principle in maintaining high-quality geospatial data:

TABLE 2: The Importance of Each Principle

Principle	Explanation	Impact on Geospatial Data
Consistency	Data should follow internal rules and logic, without contradictions across different sources.	Prevents errors in analysis, ensuring results can be trusted across platforms.
Comparability	Data should be comparable across different systems, formats, and time periods.	Facilitates the integration of data from various sources, ensuring cohesive datasets for decision-making.
Transparency	Evaluation processes must be clear, and methodologies documented for verification.	Promotes accountability and trust, ensuring data quality assessments can be reviewed and audited.

EXPLANATION OF KEY PRINCIPLES WITH TABLES

1. CONSISTENCY

- **Consistency** ensures that data values are logically consistent within themselves and across different datasets.
- Example: If data is about **building heights** in two regions, **consistent data** would ensure that height is represented uniformly, regardless of the region or the method of data collection.

TABLE 3: Example of Consistent Data

Region	Building Height (Meters)	Data Consistency Check
Region A	150	Matches defined standards and rules.
Region B	150	Matches defined standards and rules.

2. COMPARABILITY

- **Comparability** ensures that datasets from different sources or collection methods can be evaluated against each other, providing meaningful comparISOns.
- Example: **Geospatial data** from **satellite imagery** can be compared to **ground-level survey data** if both use the same measurement units and data accuracy benchmarks.

TABLE 4: Example of Comparability

Dataset	Source	Measurement Unit	Data Quality Rating
Satellite Imagery	Remote Sensing	Meters	High
Ground Survey	Field Survey	Meters	Medium

3. TRANSPARENCY

- **Transparency** ensures that the data quality evaluation process is fully documented, with **methodologies** clearly outlined. This promotes **accountability** and allows stakeholders to trust the data being evaluated.
- Example: A **geospatial dataset** about **land use** should be accompanied by a clear explanation of the **data collection method** and the **evaluation metrics** used to assess its quality.

TABLE 5: Example of Transparent Reporting

Dataset	Quality Evaluation Method	Evaluation Result	Notes
Land Use Dataset	Visual Inspection + Sampling	Accuracy 90%	Based on field data sampling.
Elevation Dataset	GPS Survey + Satellite Imagery	Positional Accuracy 98%	Verified with ground control.

SUMMARY

In conclusion, the principles of **consistency**, **comparability**, and **transparency** are essential in ensuring **geospatial data** meets high-quality standards. By following the **standardized guidelines** outlined in ISO 19157:2023, organizations can achieve data that is **reliable**, **trustworthy**, and **fit for decision-making**. The inclusion of **tables** above visually highlights the importance of each principle in maintaining **high-quality data** and supports the practical application of the standard's guidelines.

APPLYING THE PRINCIPLES IN PRACTICE

HOW TO ALIGN YOUR ORGANIZATION'S DATA QUALITY EVALUATION WITH THESE PRINCIPLES

Aligning your organization's **data quality evaluation** with the principles outlined in **ISO 19157:2023** ensures that your geospatial data is **consistent**, **comparable**, and **transparent**, thereby improving its reliability and usefulness for decision-making. Here's how to apply each principle in practice:

1. ALIGNING WITH CONSISTENCY

- **Define Data Standards**: Establish **clear, standardized rules** for how data should be collected, formatted, and represented. For example, ensure that all **geospatial datasets** use the same **coordinate system** or **measurement units**.
- **Data Validation**: Implement **validation checks** that automatically flag inconsistencies in data. This could include range checks (e.g., ensuring

building heights do not exceed expected limits) or logic checks (e.g., verifying that temporal data does not contradict chronological order).

- **Consistent Data Collection Methodologies**: Ensure that data collection is conducted using **standard methods**. This might involve **survey protocols**, **sensor calibration standards**, or **remote sensing techniques** that ensure **uniformity** across all data collected.

2. ALIGNING WITH COMPARABILITY

- **Harmonize Data Sources**: Establish procedures that ensure **data from different sources** can be compared meaningfully. For example, if using **satellite imagery** alongside **ground survey data**, ensure both datasets are recorded in the same **measurement units** and **data accuracy benchmarks**.
- **Data Normalization**: Standardize data formats, **coordinate systems**, and **spatial resolutions** to ensure that data can be easily integrated across systems and platforms. This makes combining data from multiple sources seamless.
- **Common Reporting Metrics**: Use a **unified framework** to report data quality across different datasets. Having consistent evaluation metrics allows stakeholders to **compare data quality** across projects and departments.

3. ALIGNING WITH TRANSPARENCY

- **Document Data Quality Assessment Methods**: Ensure that the methods used to assess data quality are fully **documented** and accessible. This includes the specific **quality measures** used, the **sampling techniques** applied, and the **evaluation processes** followed.
- **Provide Clear Metadata**: Every dataset should be accompanied by **metadata** that explains how data was collected, its accuracy, and the methods used for data quality evaluation. This ensures that **users** can trust the data, knowing exactly how it was obtained and assessed.
- **Engage Stakeholders**: Involve all relevant stakeholders in the **data evaluation process**, ensuring they understand the **evaluation criteria** and have access to the **results**. This could include **internal teams**, **external contractors**, or **regulatory bodies** that may rely on your data for decision-making.

BENEFITS OF STANDARDIZED DATA QUALITY LANGUAGE AND TRACEABILITY

Standardizing data quality language and ensuring **traceability** throughout the evaluation process offers numerous benefits:

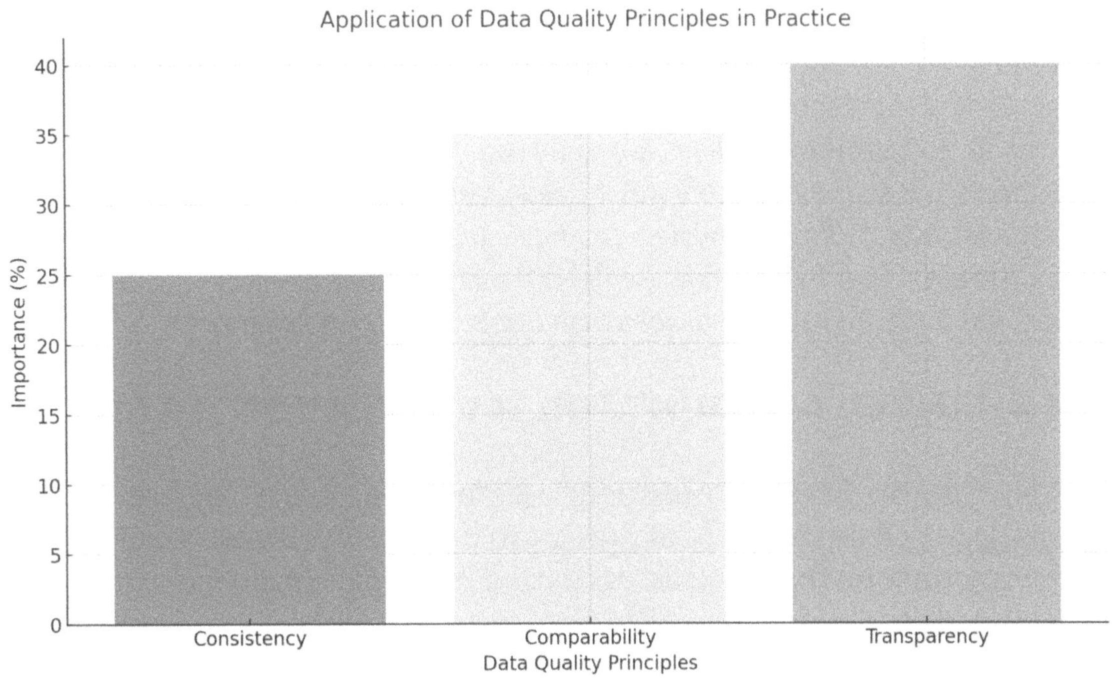

1. CONSISTENCY ACROSS ORGANIZATIONAL UNITS

- **Uniform Terminology**: Adopting **standardized data quality terminology** across your organization ensures that everyone—regardless of department or role—understands key concepts such as **accuracy**, **completeness**, and **usability** in the same way. This creates a **common language** that simplifies communication and data sharing.
- **Reduced Ambiguity**: A **standardized approach** eliminates confusion and ambiguity when discussing data quality, ensuring that evaluations, reporting, and decision-making are based on **clear, agreed-upon criteria**.

2. IMPROVED DATA INTEGRATION AND INTEROPERABILITY

- **Seamless Data Sharing**: With a common **data quality language**, datasets from different departments or even external organizations can be evaluated using the same criteria. This improves **interoperability** and makes it easier to **integrate** data from various sources without significant preprocessing.

3. BETTER DECISION-MAKING AND TRANSPARENCY

- **Improved Confidence**: When the **evaluation process** is transparent and consistent, stakeholders have more confidence in the **data quality**. This is critical for **informed decision-making**, where the quality of data directly impacts the success of policies, business strategies, or scientific outcomes.
- **Auditability**: **Traceability** ensures that data quality evaluations are **auditable**. This means that decisions made based on data can be reviewed, and the methods used to assess data quality can be verified.

4. ENHANCED ACCOUNTABILITY AND AUDIT TRAILS

- **Clear Audit Trails**: **Traceability** in the data quality evaluation process provides a **clear record** of all quality assessments. This allows organizations to track **data changes** and assess the quality of data at any point in time.
- **Regulatory Compliance**: For industries governed by regulations (e.g., environmental agencies or urban planning), having **traceable data quality processes** ensures compliance with legal and **regulatory standards**, and makes audits much easier and more transparent.

SUMMARY

In practice, applying the **principles of consistency**, **comparability**, and **transparency** ensures that data quality is maintained across all stages of data collection, processing, and reporting. Standardized **data quality language** and **traceability** not only improve **internal workflows** but also facilitate **data sharing**, **global collaboration**, and **trustworthy decision-making**. By aligning your organization's data quality evaluation with these principles, you ensure that the data you rely on for decisions is **consistent**, **reliable**, and **fit for its intended purpose**.

CHAPTER 3

Data Quality Elements and Their Application

THE SIX DATA QUALITY ELEMENTS

In **ISO 19157:2023**, the evaluation of **data quality** is based on six key **data quality elements**, as outlined in **Clause 6.5** and **Annex A** of the standard. These elements are critical for assessing the **fitness** of geospatial data for use in **decision-making, analysis**, and **operations**.

The six core data quality elements are:

1. **Completeness**
2. **Logical Consistency**
3. **Positional Accuracy**
4. **Temporal Accuracy**
5. **Thematic Accuracy**
6. **Usability**

Each element provides a framework for evaluating how well a dataset meets specific quality criteria, ensuring that data can be trusted, integrated, and applied across various systems and sectors.

1. COMPLETENESS

Completeness refers to the extent to which all required data is present. It measures whether all the **necessary** data for a specific application is available and **not missing**.

Examples of Completeness:

- **Missing values**: Incomplete datasets may have missing geographical features or attributes.
- **Empty fields**: Certain data fields might not be populated with the correct information.

Importance:

- **Inconsistent data** or **missing data** can lead to **biased** or **incorrect analyses**.
- **Completeness** is crucial for **data integration**, as incomplete data cannot be reliably combined with other datasets, leading to **decision-making errors**.

2. LOGICAL CONSISTENCY

Logical consistency assesses whether the data adheres to predefined rules and is **internally consistent**. It checks for **data integrity** across different datasets.

Examples of Logical Consistency:

- **Topological consistency**: In a map of road networks, all roads should connect properly, without ISOlated segments.
- **Data type consistency**: The data type of a value (e.g., an attribute like "elevation") should match the expected format (e.g., numeric value).

Importance:

- Ensures **data correctness** and prevents errors when integrating or comparing datasets from different sources.
- Logical consistency ensures that geospatial data reflects **real-world relationships** correctly.

3. POSITIONAL ACCURACY

Positional accuracy measures how closely the location of features in a dataset matches their **true location** on the Earth's surface.

Examples of Positional Accuracy:

- For a point feature (e.g., a building), positional accuracy indicates how close its recorded coordinates are to the actual coordinates on a map or the ground.

Importance:

- **High positional accuracy** ensures that geospatial data can be used reliably for **location-based decisions**, such as urban planning or infrastructure development.
- Inaccurate positioning can lead to **misalignment** of layers in GIS systems, causing **critical errors** in applications like navigation or land management.

4. TEMPORAL ACCURACY

Temporal accuracy assesses whether the data reflects the **correct time-related information** and whether the **time stamps** associated with the data are accurate.

Examples of Temporal Accuracy:

- **Time stamps** for satellite images may show the **exact time** a particular image was captured.
- **Longitudinal data** in environmental studies must reflect **time-related changes** accurately.

Importance:

- **Temporal accuracy** is crucial for **monitoring** and **tracking changes** over time. Inaccurate temporal data can lead to **misinterpretations** of how conditions change over periods.
- It is essential for **time-sensitive applications** such as **disaster response** or **weather forecasting**.

5. THEMATIC ACCURACY

Thematic accuracy refers to how well the **attributes** or **labels** of the dataset match the real-world phenomena they represent.

Examples of Thematic Accuracy:

- A **land use map** accurately labeling areas as **residential**, **commercial**, or **industrial**.
- **Vegetation types** correctly labeled based on the actual classification of land cover.

Importance:

- **High thematic accuracy** ensures that the data accurately represents the **real-world phenomena** it is intended to describe.
- It is critical for applications where precise categorization of features impacts **policy-making** or **environmental management**.

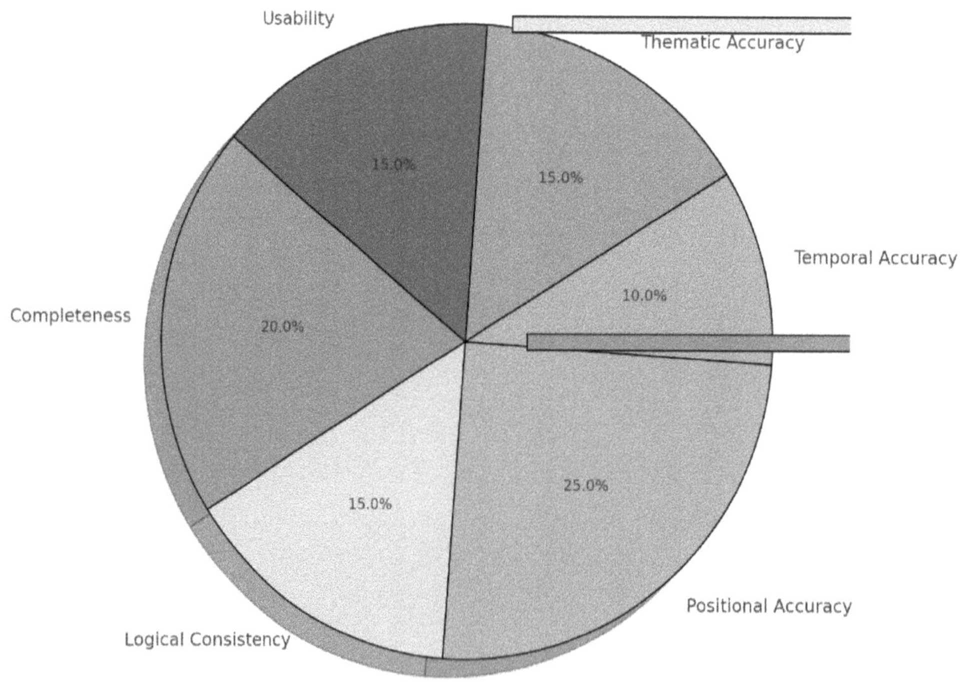

6. USABILITY

Usability refers to the extent to which the data is **fit for its intended purpose**. It evaluates how **easy** it is to use the dataset for its designated application.

Examples of Usability:

- **Metadata**: Well-documented datasets that include information on how the data was collected, processed, and can be used effectively.
- **Data format**: Data that is easily accessible and compatible with standard software tools for processing.

Importance:

- Data that is **not usable**—whether because of poor documentation, incompatible formats, or missing attributes—limits its **effectiveness** in **decision-making**.
- **Usability** ensures that users can **quickly apply the data** to solve real-world problems without extensive preprocessing.

TABLE 1: Data Quality Elements and Their Importance

Data Quality Element	Definition	Importance
Completeness	Measures the presence or absence of required data	Ensures that all needed data is available for comprehensive analysis
Logical Consistency	Ensures data follows defined rules and maintains integrity	Helps avoid errors and discrepancies when combining or comparing data
Positional Accuracy	Measures the proximity of data features to their real-world locations	Ensures data is geospatially accurate and can be used for precise location-based tasks
Temporal Accuracy	Ensures data reflects correct time-related information	Vital for time-sensitive applications, like monitoring and tracking changes
Thematic Accuracy	Measures how well data labels or attributes match real-world features	Ensures correct categorization and representation of real-world phenomena
Usability	Assesses how fit the data is for its intended use	Ensures the data is practical and can be easily used for decision-making

PRACTICAL EXAMPLE OF DATA QUALITY ELEMENTS APPLICATION

Consider a **disaster response** application where geospatial data is used to **identify flood-prone areas**. The application must meet the following criteria to ensure reliable results:

- **Completeness**: Ensure all flood-prone areas are covered in the dataset, with no gaps in coverage.
- **Logical Consistency**: Ensure that all flood boundaries follow **topological rules**, with no disconnected or incorrect segments.
- **Positional Accuracy**: Ensure that the locations of flood boundaries are accurate, matching ground truth or official maps.
- **Temporal Accuracy**: The data must be up-to-date, representing the current state of flood risks.
- **Thematic Accuracy**: Ensure that land use or zoning data is correctly labeled, so flood zones are accurately identified within urban, agricultural, or residential areas.
- **Usability**: The data should be in a format that can be easily processed by response teams using common GIS software.

SUMMARY

The six **data quality elements—completeness, logical consistency, positional accuracy, temporal accuracy, thematic accuracy**, and **usability**—are critical for assessing the **fitness** of geospatial data for its intended use. By ensuring these elements meet the highest standards, organizations can ensure that their data is **reliable, accurate**, and **usable** in real-world applications, leading to more informed decision-making and effective outcomes.

HOW TO APPLY EACH DATA QUALITY ELEMENT

Applying each of the six **data quality elements** outlined in **ISO 19157:2023** ensures that **geospatial data** meets the necessary **standards** for accuracy, consistency, and usability. This section will cover **methods for evaluating** and **reporting on each element**, along with **practical examples** of how these elements are applied to common **geospatial data challenges**.

1. COMPLETENESS

Method for Evaluating Completeness

To evaluate **completeness**, the first step is to **define the expected data coverage**. This means understanding what **data features** should be present in the dataset and comparing them to what is actually included. You can use **spatial sampling** and **visual inspections** to identify **missing features** or **incomplete attributes**.

Reporting on Completeness:

- Create a **completeness report** that specifies which data features or attributes are missing or incomplete. For example, if a land use dataset is missing **residential areas**, that would be documented.
- The report should include the **extent** of missing data, the **impact** on overall analysis, and recommendations for data completion.

Example of Applying Completeness in Geospatial Data Challenges

In **urban planning**, a city's **zoning map** may be missing **green spaces** in certain areas. To ensure completeness, the **data evaluator** would identify areas where green space is not marked and include this missing information to complete the dataset.

2. LOGICAL CONSISTENCY

Method for Evaluating Logical Consistency

Evaluating **logical consistency** involves **validating the relationships** between data elements. For example, a **topological validation** tool can be used to ensure that **roads** in a transportation dataset do not have **ISOlated segments** or that **boundaries** align properly.

Reporting on Logical Consistency:

- The report will highlight any **inconsistencies**, such as **incorrect feature connections** or **violations** of predefined rules (e.g., overlapping polygons for land parcels).

- It should explain how these inconsistencies affect **data quality** and the **accuracy** of analyses.

Example of Applying Logical Consistency in Geospatial Data Challenges

In **mapping flood zones**, **logical consistency** is necessary to ensure that **flood boundaries** do not overlap incorrectly with **urban areas** or **water bodies**. Inconsistent data could lead to **inaccurate flood risk assessments**, especially in high-risk areas.

3. POSITIONAL ACCURACY

Method for Evaluating Positional Accuracy

Positional accuracy is assessed by comparing the **coordinates** of **data features** (e.g., building locations, roads) against **ground truth** or **higher-accuracy datasets**. This can be done using **GPS measurements** or **remote sensing data** for comparISOn.

Reporting on Positional Accuracy:

- The **positional accuracy report** should include the **error margin** between the measured position and the true position.
- Report the **acceptable range** of errors and the **impact** on applications (e.g., **navigation, surveying**).

Example of Applying Positional Accuracy in Geospatial Data Challenges

For a **navigation system** that provides **real-time directions**, high **positional accuracy** is essential. A **building footprint** dataset should be compared against **GPS data** or high-resolution **satellite imagery** to ensure the accuracy of **location data** for users relying on precise directions.

4. TEMPORAL ACCURACY

Method for Evaluating Temporal Accuracy

To assess **temporal accuracy**, compare the **time stamps** associated with the data against **real-world time events** (e.g., when an image was captured or when a survey was conducted). Temporal errors can arise from **data outdatedness** or mismatched time references.

Reporting on Temporal Accuracy:

- **Report any discrepancies** between **data timestamps** and **real-world events**.
- The report should include how **outdated data** might affect analyses and decisions, especially in time-sensitive applications.

Example of Applying Temporal Accuracy in Geospatial Data Challenges

In **environmental monitoring**, accurate **temporal data** is crucial. For example, the **change in land cover** (e.g., deforestation) must be assessed based on **recent data** from **satellite imagery** or **field surveys**. Using **outdated data** could lead to inaccurate predictions about land use changes and **environmental risks**.

5. THEMATIC ACCURACY

Method for Evaluating Thematic Accuracy

Thematic accuracy is evaluated by checking whether the **data attributes** (e.g., land use classification, vegetation types) correctly represent the real-world phenomena they are supposed to describe. **Field verification**, **comparISOn with reference datasets**, and **expert validation** can be used to assess thematic accuracy.

Reporting on Thematic Accuracy:

- The report should include any **mismatched attributes**, such as incorrectly labeled land types or vegetation classes.
- Provide a **corrective action plan** for fixing **misclassified features**.

Example of Applying Thematic Accuracy in Geospatial Data Challenges

In a **land use mapping** project, if **agricultural areas** are mistakenly labeled as **urban zones**, this will impact land-use policy and **urban planning** decisions. Evaluating and correcting **thematic accuracy** is critical to ensure the correct classification of land for effective **resource management**.

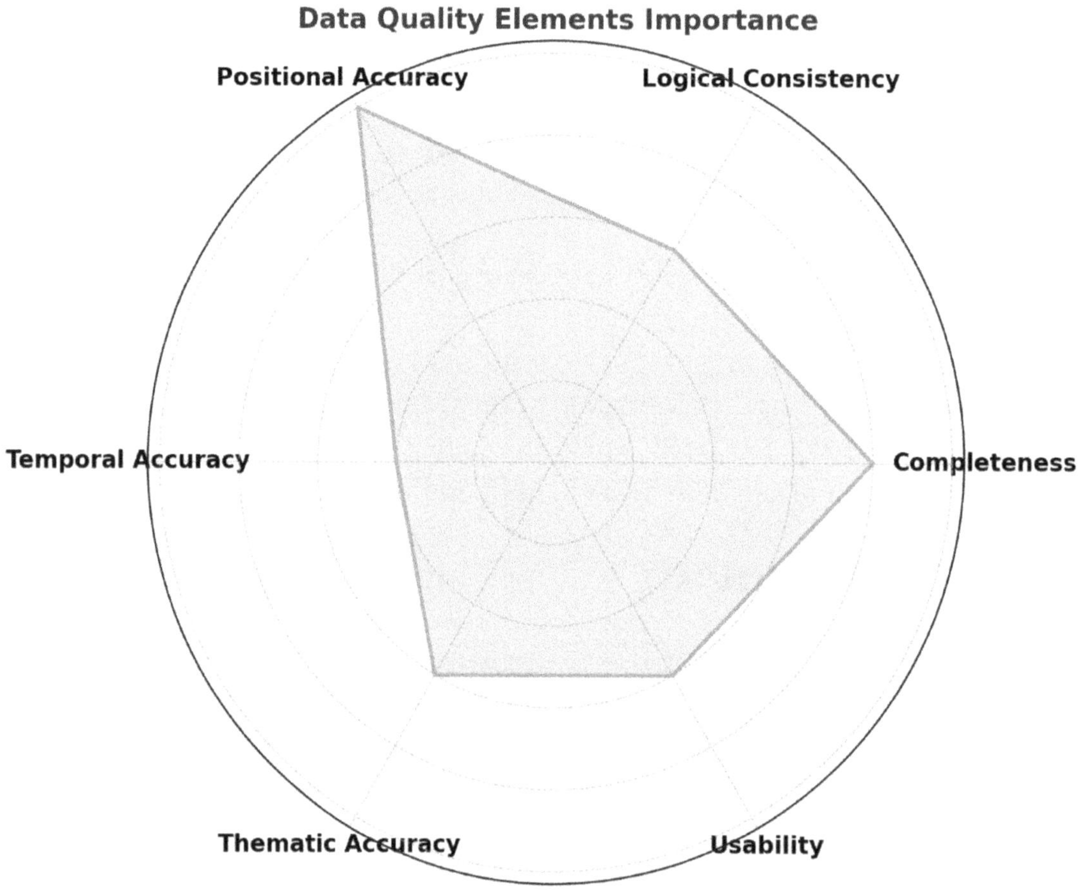

6. USABILITY

Method for Evaluating Usability

Usability is assessed by determining whether the dataset is **fit for its intended purpose**. This includes checking **metadata completeness**, **data formats**, and whether the data is **easy to access and interpret**.

Reporting on Usability:

- The **usability report** should provide feedback on **data accessibility** (e.g., whether it is in the correct format) and whether **documentation** is available to guide users in applying the data effectively.
- It should also include recommendations for improving **data usability**, such as ensuring that the dataset is compatible with commonly used software tools.

Example of Applying Usability in Geospatial Data Challenges

For a **disaster response** team relying on **real-time geospatial data** to track evacuation routes, data usability is crucial. If the data is difficult to access, or poorly documented, it can delay response efforts and lead to **misinterpretations**. The dataset must be easily downloadable, clearly labeled, and compatible with **GIS software**.

SUMMARY

To effectively apply the **data quality elements** outlined in **ISO 19157:2023**, organizations must **evaluate** and **report** on the six key aspects: **completeness**, **logical consistency**, **positional accuracy**, **temporal accuracy**, **thematic accuracy**, and **usability**. These evaluations ensure that geospatial data is **fit for its intended purpose** and can be confidently used in **decision-making** across various sectors, including **urban planning**, **environmental management**, and **disaster response**. By understanding and applying these elements, organizations can improve the **quality** of their data and **reduce risks** in their operations.

ALIGNING EVALUATION WITH ORGANIZATIONAL GOALS

Aligning the **evaluation of data quality** with an organization's **goals** and **data governance objectives** is essential for ensuring that **data quality practices** are effective and contribute directly to the **success of organizational strategies**. Proper alignment ensures that the organization's data supports its operational, strategic, and regulatory requirements.

Here's how to tailor the evaluation process to meet organizational **data governance objectives**:

1. DEFINE CLEAR DATA GOVERNANCE OBJECTIVES

Before aligning the evaluation process, the first step is to clearly define **data governance objectives** that align with the organization's overall goals. These could include:

- **Improving Decision-Making**: Ensuring that the data is of **high quality** to support **informed decisions**.
- **Compliance and Regulatory Adherence**: Meeting **industry regulations**, **legal requirements**, and **privacy standards** through data governance.
- **Operational Efficiency**: Enabling the organization to use data efficiently and cost-effectively, avoiding **data duplication** and reducing errors.
- **Data Integration**: Ensuring that data can be **easily integrated** across different systems within the organization.

Once these goals are clear, the **data quality evaluation process** can be shaped to meet these needs.

2. ALIGN DATA QUALITY ELEMENTS WITH BUSINESS OBJECTIVES

Each of the **six data quality elements** should be aligned with specific organizational goals. Here's how:

- **Completeness**:
  - **Business Goal**: Ensure the dataset has all necessary components to **support business processes**. For example, a **customer database** needs complete contact information for better communication.
  - **Evaluation Approach**: Regularly audit datasets to ensure no critical data is missing, and establish guidelines for **mandatory fields** (e.g., names, addresses).
- **Logical Consistency**:
  - **Business Goal**: Maintain data integrity across multiple departments and systems.
  - **Evaluation Approach**: Use **topological validation** to ensure **rules** are adhered to across various datasets, such as ensuring that **customer records** do not have conflicting information.
- **Positional Accuracy**:
  - **Business Goal**: Ensure that geographic data is accurate for **location-based decisions**, such as **site selection** or **asset management**.

    - **Evaluation Approach**: Compare data against **ground truth** or high-accuracy datasets (e.g., **GPS** or **satellite imagery**) to assess accuracy.
- **Temporal Accuracy**:
    - **Business Goal**: Keep data up to date to ensure relevance, particularly for applications that rely on **time-sensitive data**, such as **supply chain management** or **inventory systems**.
    - **Evaluation Approach**: Ensure that data has **accurate timestamps**, and monitor the **recency** of datasets to avoid using outdated information.
- **Thematic Accuracy**:
    - **Business Goal**: Align the classification of data with organizational needs. For example, ensuring **land use maps** accurately represent **zoning regulations**.
    - **Evaluation Approach**: Regularly validate **attributes** of datasets to ensure that categories and classifications are **correct** and align with the intended use.
- **Usability**:
    - **Business Goal**: Make sure that data is **easy to access** and use for **decision-making** across the organization.
    - **Evaluation Approach**: Ensure data is **well-documented** with **clear metadata** and available in formats compatible with existing **software systems**.

3. IMPLEMENT A FLEXIBLE EVALUATION FRAMEWORK

Create a **flexible framework** that allows the organization to adapt its **data quality evaluation** based on changing business needs, technology advancements, and regulatory changes. This framework should:

- **Set Evaluation Standards**: Define the standards for each data quality element (e.g., acceptable thresholds for **accuracy** or **completeness**).
- **Customize Evaluation Metrics**: Tailor metrics based on the specific needs of different departments or business units. For example, the **marketing team** may prioritize **thematic accuracy** in customer data, while **operations** may focus on **positional accuracy**.
- **Regular Reviews**: Ensure that data quality evaluation is **reviewed periodically** to keep it aligned with **organizational changes** and external factors (e.g., market conditions or legal requirements).

4. ALIGN WITH DATA GOVERNANCE ROLES AND RESPONSIBILITIES

Ensure that the data evaluation process is closely tied to the organization's **data governance structure**. Each role within the governance framework should have clear responsibilities regarding data quality, such as:

- **Data Stewardship**: Data stewards should oversee the evaluation of data quality within specific domains, ensuring data is properly maintained and evaluated.
- **Data Quality Owners**: Individuals responsible for ensuring that data quality elements are measured and that the standards are met.
- **Governance Committees**: Committees that review overall data governance performance and ensure that data quality objectives are being met in line with organizational goals.

5. ESTABLISH DATA QUALITY PERFORMANCE INDICATORS (KPIs)

Develop **Key Performance Indicators (KPIs)** to measure the **effectiveness** of the data quality evaluation process and its alignment with the organization's goals. Example KPIs could include:

- **Accuracy Rate**: Percentage of **geospatial data** that meets positional accuracy standards.
- **Completeness Rate**: Percentage of datasets that contain all required attributes or features.
- **Consistency Compliance**: Percentage of data that adheres to predefined **logical consistency rules**.
- **Timeliness**: The percentage of data that is updated or verified within a **certain time period**.

These KPIs can be tracked over time to ensure continuous improvement and alignment with business goals.

6. INTEGRATE WITH DATA MANAGEMENT SYSTEMS

Integrating data quality evaluation into your organization's **data management systems** ensures that evaluation is embedded into daily workflows. This can be achieved by:

- **Automation**: Use **automated data quality checks** that run when data is entered, updated, or transferred across systems. This helps in real-time detection of data issues.
- **Data Governance Software**: Implement software that monitors and tracks **data quality metrics** and automatically generates reports based on predefined **evaluation criteria**.

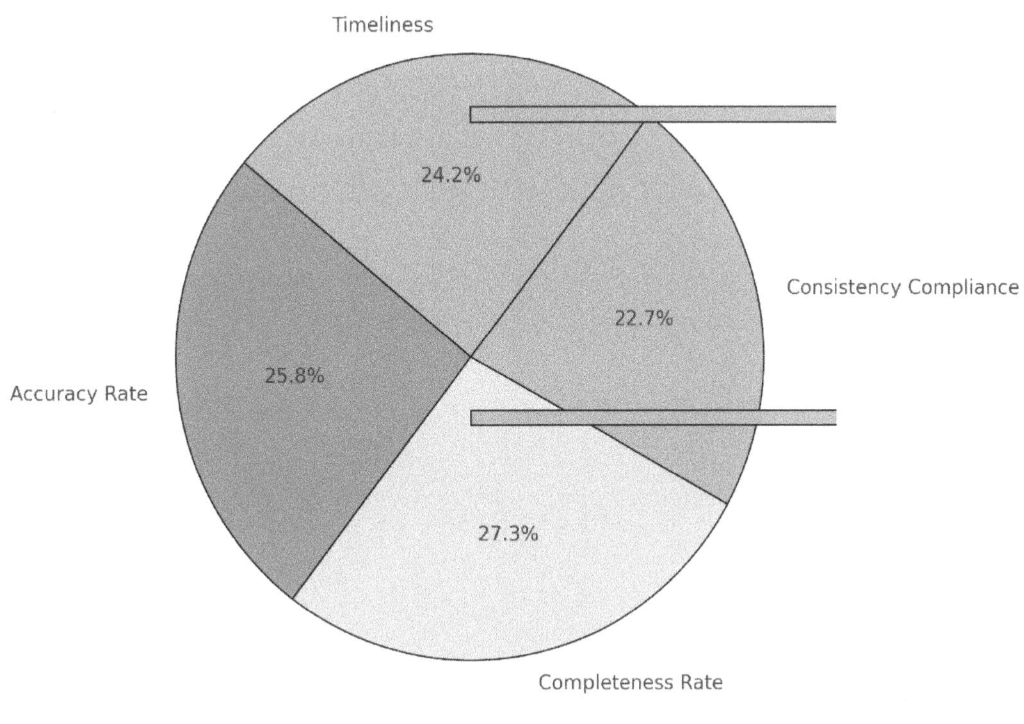

7. COMMUNICATE FINDINGS AND IMPACT

Ensure that the results of the data quality evaluation are clearly communicated to all relevant stakeholders in the organization. This could include:

- **Data Quality Dashboards**: Visual dashboards that show key metrics, making it easy for decision-makers to see the status of data quality across departments.
- **Impact Reports**: Reports that explain the **impact of poor data quality** on business outcomes and decision-making. These reports should highlight areas for improvement and suggest corrective actions.

SUMMARY

To align **data quality evaluation** with organizational goals, it's essential to tailor the evaluation process to meet **specific business objectives**, **regulatory requirements**, and **strategic initiatives**. By defining clear **data governance objectives**, integrating **evaluation frameworks**, and establishing **KPIs**, organizations can ensure that their **geospatial data** is reliable, usable, and supports **data-driven decisions**. The process should be flexible and adaptable to **changing organizational needs**, ensuring that data quality remains at the forefront of business operations.

CHAPTER 4

The Evaluation and Reporting Process

SAMPLING AND EVALUATION METHODS (CLAUSE 6.3)

In **ISO 19157:2023**, **sampling** is a key method for evaluating the **quality of geospatial data**. Clause 6.3 defines **sampling methods** that are critical for ensuring that evaluations are **representative**, **efficient**, and aligned with **data quality standards**.

Sampling involves selecting a subset of the total dataset to evaluate its quality, rather than analyzing every single data point. This makes the **evaluation process** more **practical** and **cost-effective**, especially when dealing with **large datasets** or **complex geospatial information**.

1. THE ROLE OF SAMPLING IN ENSURING DATA QUALITY

Sampling plays an essential role in ensuring the **reliability** and **representativeness** of data quality evaluations. Here's why it is crucial:

Efficiency and Cost-Effectiveness

- **Sampling** reduces the need to evaluate **entire datasets**, which may be impractical due to time, budget, or resource constraints.
- Evaluating a **random or stratified sample** provides a **statistically valid** way to assess the quality of the data without the overhead of analyzing every single data point.

Ensures Statistical Validity

- By using **representative samples**, organizations can **generalize results** to the entire dataset. Sampling allows for valid **inferences** about the data quality of the entire dataset based on the quality of the sample.
- It ensures that data quality assessments are **accurate**, even when dealing with large-scale datasets.

Identifies Potential Issues

- Sampling allows organizations to identify data quality issues that may not be apparent when only evaluating small subsets of data. For example, if a **sample** of geospatial data reveals **positional inaccuracies**, this may indicate broader issues across the entire dataset.

Compliance with Standards

- **ISO 19157:2023** encourages sampling to be conducted using **standardized methods** that ensure data quality evaluation meets international requirements for consistency and comparability.

2. HOW TO PLAN AND IMPLEMENT REPRESENTATIVE SAMPLING

To effectively implement **representative sampling**, the following steps should be taken:

Step 1: Define the Sampling Objective

First, define the **purpose** of the sampling process and what you aim to achieve. Examples of sampling objectives include:

- **Assessing Accuracy**: Evaluate the **positional accuracy** of geospatial features in a dataset.
- **Identifying Completeness**: Determine whether all required attributes are present in a dataset.

Once the objective is clear, determine what **data quality elements** need to be evaluated (e.g., completeness, logical consistency, positional accuracy).

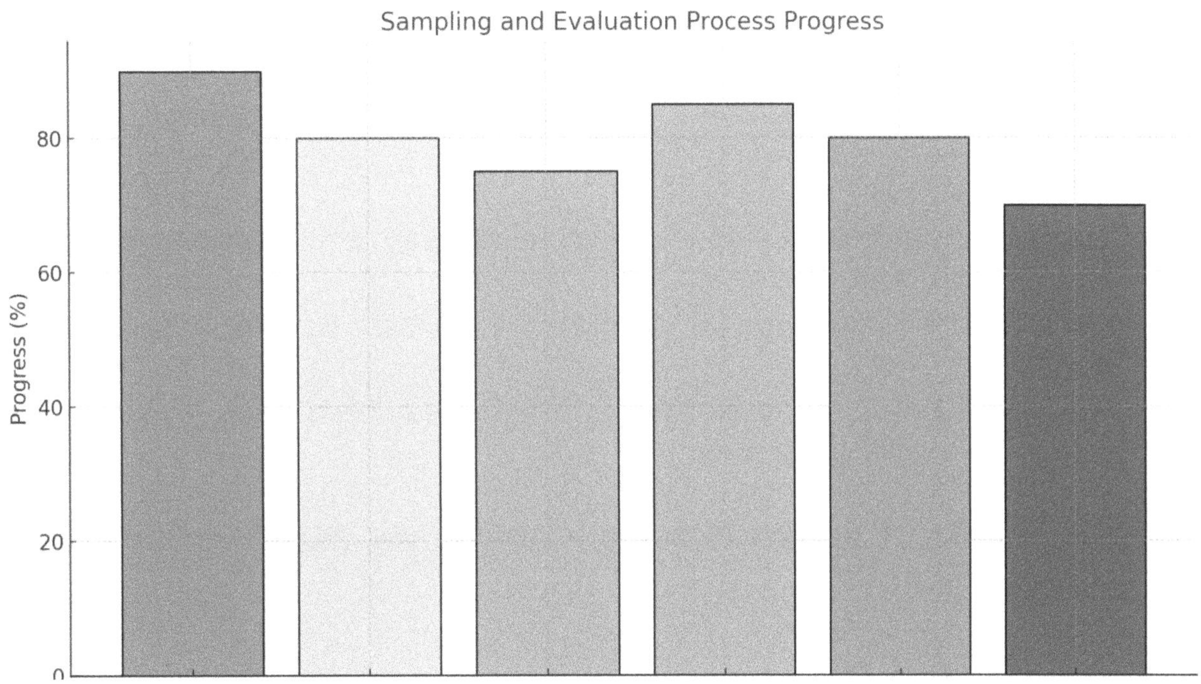

Step 2: Choose the Sampling Method

Several sampling methods can be used, depending on the nature of the data and the objective. Common methods include:

- **Random Sampling**: This method selects **random points** or features from the dataset to ensure that every element has an equal chance of being selected. This is ideal for datasets where **each data point** is equally important.
- **Stratified Sampling**: This method divides the data into **distinct strata or categories** and then samples from each stratum. This is useful for datasets with **multiple categories** (e.g., land use types, elevation zones) to ensure that each category is represented.
- **Systematic Sampling**: In this method, samples are taken at **regular intervals** throughout the dataset. This can be useful for **spatially distributed data** (e.g., satellite imagery data at fixed intervals).

- **Cluster Sampling**: This method involves dividing the data into **clusters** and then randomly selecting some clusters for evaluation. This method is useful for large datasets with geographic or thematic clusters.

Step 3: Determine Sample Size

The **sample size** should be large enough to provide a **statistically valid** evaluation but small enough to be manageable. The sample size can be determined based on factors like:

- **Desired Confidence Level**: A higher confidence level typically requires a larger sample size.
- **Data Size**: The total size of the dataset influences how many samples are needed.
- **Margin of Error**: A smaller margin of error requires a larger sample size to ensure the results are precise.

Statistical formulas or software tools can be used to calculate the optimal sample size based on these factors.

Step 4: Collect and Evaluate the Sample

Once the sample is selected, evaluate its quality based on the selected data quality elements (e.g., **positional accuracy**, **completeness**). The evaluation could involve:

- **Field verification** for positional accuracy.
- **ComparISOn with reference datasets** for thematic accuracy.
- **Use of automated tools** for consistency checks (e.g., logical consistency validation in GIS software).

Step 5: Report Findings and Extrapolate Results

After evaluating the sample, summarize the findings and extrapolate the results to the full dataset. The report should include:

- **Findings**: Document any **data quality issues** identified in the sample, such as missing data, inconsistencies, or inaccuracies.

- **Sampling Methodology**: Provide details about how the sample was selected, the sample size, and the sampling method used.
- **Data Quality Extrapolation**: Based on the sample evaluation, extrapolate the results to estimate the **overall quality** of the dataset (e.g., the expected level of **positional accuracy** for the entire dataset).
- **Recommendations**: Provide actionable recommendations for improving the dataset, if necessary.

3. EXAMPLE OF SAMPLING IN GEOSPATIAL DATA EVALUATION

Example 1: Positional Accuracy in Land Parcel Mapping

In a geospatial dataset representing **land parcels**, you want to evaluate the **positional accuracy** of the data. Here's how you might apply sampling:

1. **Sampling Objective**: Assess the positional accuracy of land parcels.
2. **Sampling Method**: Use **random sampling** to select 100 land parcel points from the dataset.
3. **Sample Size**: Choose a sample size based on the total number of parcels and the desired confidence level.
4. **Evaluation**: For each selected parcel, compare its **GPS coordinates** with the actual positions identified using **satellite imagery** or **ground truth data**.
5. **Reporting**: Provide a report on the positional accuracy, indicating how much of the dataset meets the acceptable positional accuracy standards and extrapolate the findings to the whole dataset.

In ISO 19157:2023, sampling **is a critical tool for evaluating the** quality **of** geospatial data **in a** cost-effective and statistically valid **manner. By selecting the appropriate** sampling method, **determining the** sample size, **and conducting** comprehensive evaluations, **organizations can ensure that data quality assessments are** representative **of the entire dataset. Implementing** well-planned sampling strategies **helps organizations achieve more** reliable **and** efficient data quality evaluations, **ensuring that their data supports** informed decision-making **across various domains.**

BEST PRACTICES FOR DOCUMENTING AND ENSURING REPRODUCIBILITY IN DATA EVALUATION

To ensure that **data evaluation** is both **transparent** and **reproducible**, organizations must establish **documentation practices** and methodologies that guarantee that any data quality evaluation process can be consistently repeated with the same results. Adhering to best practices for documentation and reproducibility helps build **trust** in the data and the processes used to assess it.

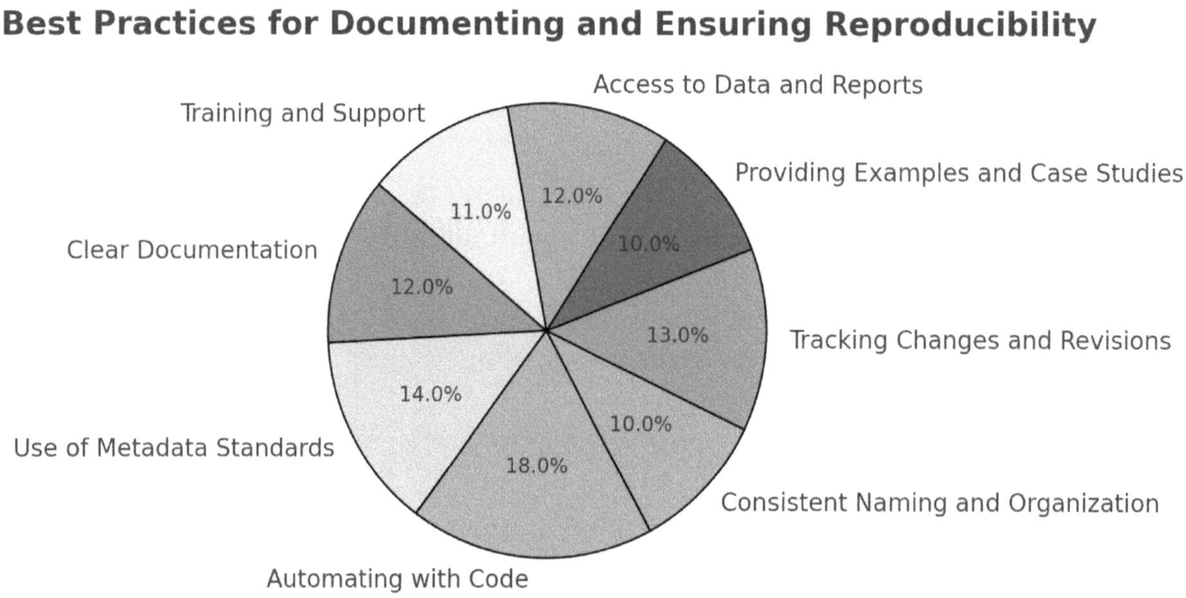

1. CLEARLY DOCUMENT DATA QUALITY EVALUATION METHODS

Why it's important:

Proper documentation allows users and stakeholders to understand how data quality was assessed and ensures that the process can be **repeated** with **identical conditions**.

Best Practices:

- **Methodology Transparency**: Clearly document the **sampling techniques** (e.g., random, stratified), the **criteria used for evaluation**, and the **tools** (e.g., GIS software, data validation scripts) used during the evaluation.
- **Detailed Data Collection Procedures**: Outline the exact steps followed when collecting the sample data, ensuring anyone can replicate the data collection process without ambiguity.
- **Tools and Versions**: Record the specific **software versions** (e.g., GIS tools, Python libraries) and **scripts** used to process and evaluate the data.
- **Data Quality Criteria**: List the exact thresholds, formulas, or metrics used to evaluate data elements like **completeness**, **accuracy**, and **consistency**.

2. USE METADATA AND DOCUMENTATION STANDARDS

Why it's important:

Metadata is essential for describing **how** and **why** data was collected and evaluated. Well-documented metadata ensures that **others can understand, reuse**, and **validate** the data evaluation process.

Best Practices:

- **Standardized Metadata Formats**: Use standard formats such as **ISO 19115** or **FGDC metadata standards** to document data quality assessment, including details like **spatial reference systems**, **data collection methods**, and **quality metrics**.
- **Data Provenance**: Track and document **data provenance**, including **source** (where the data came from), **history** (how the data has been modified), and **versioning** (when updates occurred). This allows for tracing any data quality issues back to their origin.
- **Quality Assessment Reports**: Include a section in your metadata that specifically outlines the **methods used** to evaluate the data, including **sampling techniques**, **evaluation criteria**, and **validation procedures**.

3. AUTOMATE REPRODUCIBILITY WITH CODE AND SCRIPTS

Why it's important:

Reproducibility is enhanced when the entire evaluation process, from data collection to quality assessment, is fully automated. Code and scripts ensure that the exact same methodology can be applied without errors or discrepancies.

Best Practices:

- **Version Control**: Use **version control systems** (e.g., Git) to track changes to scripts and documentation over time, ensuring that anyone can access previous versions of the evaluation process.
- **Automated Data Processing**: Write **reusable scripts** (e.g., in Python, R, or SQL) that automate data cleaning, sampling, and evaluation steps, making it easy to reproduce evaluations.
- **Clear Instructions**: Provide clear, step-by-step **documentation** on how to use the scripts, including dependencies (e.g., libraries, databases), input data formats, and expected output.
- **Containerization**: Consider using tools like **Docker** to create **reproducible environments** where code and data processing can be replicated across different systems or by different users.

4. USE CONSISTENT NAMING AND ORGANIZATION STANDARDS

Why it's important:

Consistency in naming conventions and data organization ensures that any person, team, or system can find and use the data, methods, and results in a standardized manner.

Best Practices:

- **Standardized File Naming**: Use **clear and consistent naming conventions** for datasets, metadata files, scripts, and reports. This should include information such as the **data version**, **date of collection**, and **data type**.
- **Folder Structure**: Organize data, scripts, and reports into clearly defined folder structures (e.g., `/data/`, `/scripts/`, `/reports/`) to help users navigate the materials easily.

- **Clear Variable Names**: Ensure that variables in datasets and scripts have **descriptive names** that clearly convey their meaning (e.g., `accuracy_positional` rather than `acc1`).

5. TRACK CHANGES AND REVISIONS

Why it's important:

Tracking changes helps maintain the **integrity** of the evaluation process. It allows users to see **how** and **why** data quality assessments may have changed over time.

Best Practices:

- **Change Logs**: Maintain **change logs** for data quality evaluation reports, metadata, and scripts, documenting any revisions or updates made to methods or findings.
- **Audit Trails**: Implement an **audit trail** system to track all changes to datasets, evaluations, and reports. This helps trace the evolution of data quality assessments and ensure accountability.
- **Versioning**: For any updated dataset, **version control** should be implemented, marking each revision and noting what changes were made.

6. PROVIDE EXAMPLES AND CASE STUDIES FOR CLARITY

Why it's important:

Providing **examples** or **case studies** illustrates how data quality evaluation methods are applied in practice, ensuring clarity for users and stakeholders.

Best Practices:

- **Sample Evaluations**: Include **sample datasets** and **evaluation reports** that show exactly how the data quality methods were applied. This makes the process more tangible and easier to follow.
- **Case Studies**: Share **real-world case studies** where data quality evaluation methods were applied successfully. This helps demonstrate the value of these processes and builds confidence in their effectiveness.

7. PROVIDE ACCESS TO DATA AND EVALUATION REPORTS

Why it's important:

Making the data and evaluation reports accessible ensures that **others can replicate** the data evaluation process and verify results independently.

Best Practices:

- **Open Access**: Whenever possible, **make datasets, scripts, and evaluation reports publicly available** or within an internal data repository.
- **Documentation in Reports**: Include detailed descriptions of **methodologies** and **findings** in reports so that anyone reviewing the evaluation can understand and reproduce the results.
- **External Review**: Consider involving an **external reviewer** or **peer review process** to validate the reproducibility and transparency of the evaluation.

8. PROVIDE TRAINING AND SUPPORT

Why it's important:

Training ensures that team members and stakeholders understand the evaluation process, the importance of data quality, and how to use the documentation and tools effectively.

Best Practices:

- **Training Sessions**: Organize **workshops** or **training sessions** to explain how data quality evaluations are carried out, including using scripts, interpreting results, and maintaining reproducibility.
- **User Guides**: Create clear and concise **user guides** and **FAQs** that explain how to follow the evaluation methods and reproduce results.

SUMMARY

To ensure that **data quality evaluation** is both **documented** and **reproducible**, organizations must follow **best practices** such as clear documentation, consistent naming conventions, version control, and providing access to data and results. By embedding these practices into your data evaluation process, you can guarantee that the process is **transparent**, **consistent**, and can be **replicated** by others, enhancing trust in your data and improving decision-making across the organization.

REPORTING DATA QUALITY INFORMATION (CLAUSE 7)

Clause 7 of **ISO 19157:2023** outlines the requirements for **reporting data quality information**. It emphasizes the need for **clear**, **transparent**, and **comprehensive** reporting on data quality evaluations to ensure that stakeholders can **understand**, **validate**, and **make informed decisions** based on the data. A well-structured quality evaluation report is essential for **reproducibility**, **transparency**, and ensuring that the data meets the **required standards** for its intended use.

1. WHAT TO INCLUDE IN A QUALITY EVALUATION REPORT

A **quality evaluation report** should be **comprehensive** and include all the relevant details that allow stakeholders to assess the **validity** and **trustworthiness** of the data quality evaluation. The key components of a report include:

1.1 Overview of Data Quality Evaluation

- **Purpose**: Provide a brief summary of the **objective** of the data quality evaluation. This includes the goals of assessing data quality and how it aligns with the overall objectives of the organization or project.
- **Scope**: Define the **scope** of the evaluation, including which **data elements** (e.g., positional accuracy, completeness, thematic accuracy) were assessed and which datasets or geographical areas were evaluated.
- **Data Sources**: List the **data sources** used in the evaluation, including any **reference datasets**, **sampling methods**, and **tools** used to assess data quality.

1.2 Evaluation Methods and Criteria

- **Sampling Methods**: Clearly describe the **sampling methodology** used, including **sampling size**, **sampling techniques** (e.g., random, stratified, systematic), and any **restrictions** or assumptions made during the sampling process.
- **Evaluation Criteria**: Provide a detailed explanation of the **criteria** used for evaluating data quality elements, such as **accuracy** thresholds for positional accuracy or acceptable error margins for thematic accuracy.
- **Tools and Techniques**: Describe the **software** or **tools** used for evaluating the data, such as **GIS software**, **statistical tools**, or **automated validation scripts**.

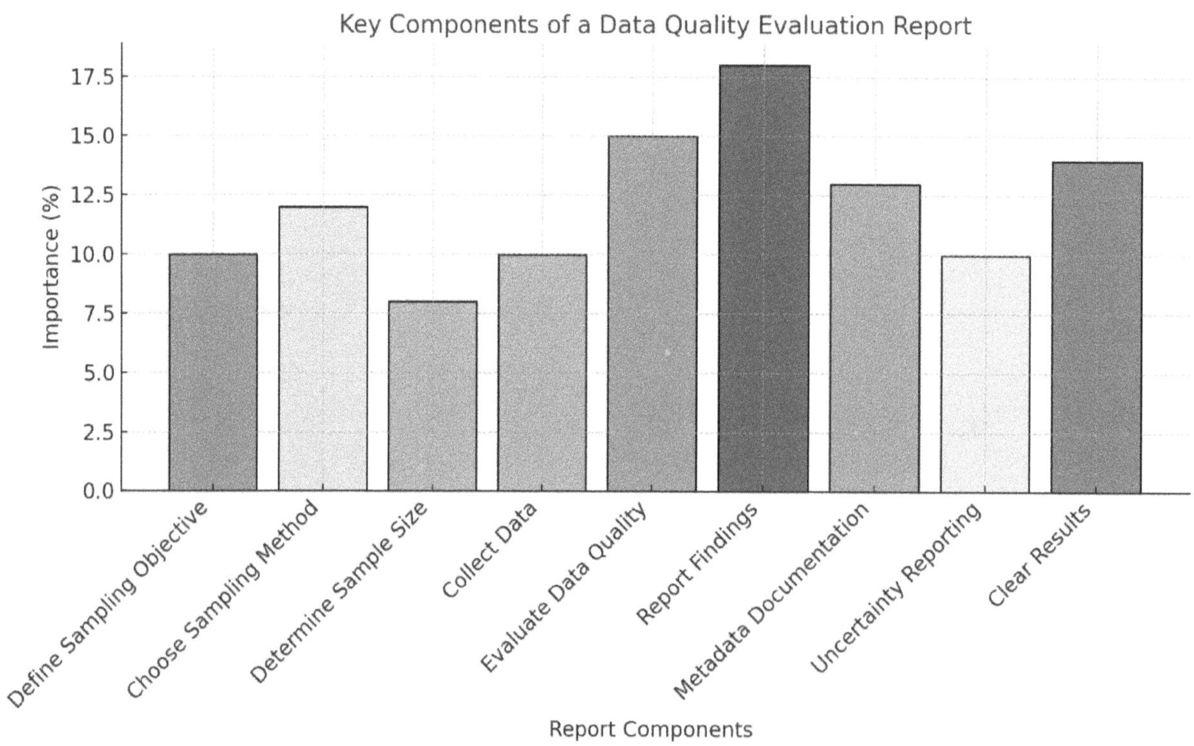

1.3 Results of Data Quality Evaluation

- **Summary of Findings**: Provide an overall summary of the findings from the evaluation. This should include **successes, issues,** and areas where the dataset met or did not meet **quality standards**.

- **Quality Metrics**: Include **quantitative data** on each quality element, such as **accuracy percentages**, **completeness percentages**, and **consistency metrics**. These metrics should be clearly defined and easy to interpret.

1.4 Metadata and Data Provenance

- **Metadata**: A key element of the report is the **metadata** associated with the data. This includes:
  - **Data source details**: Where the data came from, its version, and any transformations or modifications made.
  - **Data collection methods**: How the data was collected, including the tools, techniques, and sampling methods used.
  - **Data validation and quality checks**: Information on the checks used to assess data quality.
- **Data Provenance**: Document the **history** of the data, including **changes** or **updates** made over time, ensuring that stakeholders know the **source** and **integrity** of the data.

1.5 Uncertainty and Limitations

- **Uncertainty Reporting**: It's important to include a discussion of **uncertainty** associated with the data. This could include:
  - **Uncertainty in measurements**: Any errors or approximations inherent in the data (e.g., GPS positional error).
  - **Confidence intervals**: Indicating the **range of uncertainty** around key metrics (e.g., positional accuracy).
  - **Data gaps**: Any **missing or incomplete data** that may affect the analysis.
- **Limitations**: Outline the **limitations** of the data and the evaluation process, such as **sampling biases**, **incomplete datasets**, or constraints on evaluation methodology.

1.6 Recommendations for Data Improvement

- **Actionable Recommendations**: Based on the findings, provide **recommendations** for improving data quality. This could include:
  - **Data collection improvements**: Suggestions for improving the methodology used to collect data.

- **Data correction**: Identifying specific issues and recommending corrections to enhance data quality.

1.7 Summary and Conclusion

- **Conclusion**: Provide a concise conclusion summarizing the overall data quality evaluation, the degree to which data quality objectives were met, and whether the data is suitable for its intended use.
- **Next Steps**: Highlight any further steps needed, such as additional data quality assessments, dataset corrections, or further testing.

2. THE IMPORTANCE OF METADATA, UNCERTAINTY, AND CLEAR RESULTS

2.1 The Importance of Metadata

- **Transparency**: Metadata enhances transparency by documenting the **context** of the data, the **processes** used for its collection and evaluation, and the **quality** of the data. It allows others to understand how data was evaluated, and to reproduce or validate the evaluation process.
- **Data Usability**: Comprehensive metadata helps users understand the **limitations**, **accuracy**, and **applicability** of the data, making it easier to use effectively in decision-making.
- **Interoperability**: Well-documented metadata makes it easier to integrate and share data with other systems, ensuring that data from different sources can be combined without introducing errors or inconsistencies.

2.2 The Importance of Uncertainty

- **Informed Decision-Making**: Understanding the **uncertainty** in data quality is critical for **decision-makers**. For example, in applications like **navigation**, **spatial planning**, or **environmental monitoring**, knowing the uncertainty in positional accuracy can affect the **reliability** of decisions made from the data.
- **Risk Management**: Reporting uncertainty helps identify areas where data quality issues may impact the **outcomes** of analyses or operations. It allows organizations to plan accordingly, mitigating risks associated with **inaccurate data**.

- **Transparency and Trust**: Acknowledging uncertainty and documenting it transparently builds **trust** in the data and the processes used to assess it. It ensures that users are aware of potential data limitations and helps avoid **misinterpretation** of results.

2.3 The Importance of Clear Results

- **Clarity**: Clear results help stakeholders quickly understand the **data quality status**. This is crucial for **resource allocation**, **policy development**, and other organizational activities that rely on **data-driven decision-making**.
- **Actionable Insights**: When results are presented clearly, they provide **actionable insights** for improving data quality. Clear reporting allows teams to identify **specific issues**, prioritize solutions, and implement **corrective actions** more efficiently.

3. SAMPLE TABLE FOR REPORTING DATA QUALITY INFORMATION

Below is an example of how data quality information can be structured in a report:

TABLE 1: Sample Data Quality Report

Data Quality Element	Evaluation Method	Result	Uncertainty	Recommendations
Positional Accuracy	ComparISOn with GPS data	95% accuracy	±5 meters	Improve GPS calibration
Completeness	Visual inspection, comparISOn	98% complete	-	Add missing fields for addresses
Logical Consistency	Topological validation	99% consistent	-	Ensure consistent polygon boundaries
Thematic Accuracy	ComparISOn with reference dataset	92% accurate	±3% error	Update land-use classification
Usability	Data format compatibility check	Fully usable	-	Standardize metadata format

SUMMARY

The **data quality evaluation report** is a critical document for **transparency** and **reproducibility** in data quality assessments. It should include **metadata**, a clear description of **uncertainty**, and detailed results that are easy to interpret. By following best practices for reporting, organizations can ensure that their data quality evaluations are **transparent**, **comprehensive**, and **actionable**, facilitating informed decision-making and continuous improvement of data quality.

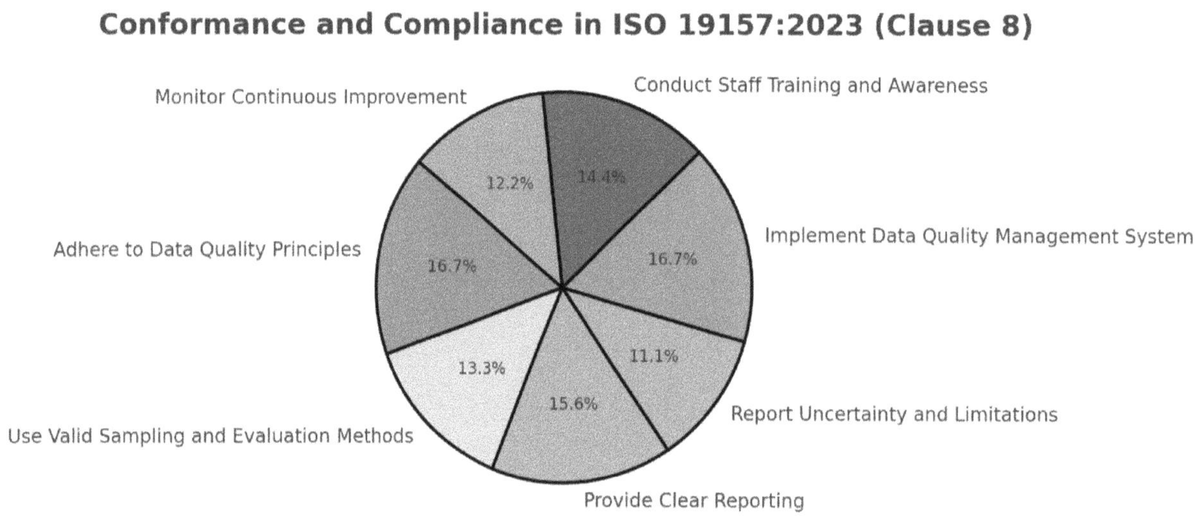

CONFORMANCE AND COMPLIANCE (CLAUSE 8)

ISO 19157:2023 provides detailed guidelines for ensuring the **quality** of **geospatial data**. **Conformance** to this standard ensures that data meets the **specified quality criteria** and can be reliably used for its intended applications. **Compliance** means adhering to these quality standards in practice, ensuring that the data can support **decision-making**, **analysis**, and other data-driven processes.

1. WHAT IT MEANS TO CONFORM TO ISO 19157:2023

Conformance to **ISO 19157:2023** means that geospatial data evaluation follows the **principles** and **procedures** outlined in the standard. To conform, an organization must demonstrate that:

1.1. Adherence to Data Quality Principles

Organizations must ensure that their **data quality evaluations** align with the **core principles** defined in **Clause 4** of the standard. These principles include:

- **Consistency**: Data must adhere to defined rules and be internally consistent.
- **Comparability**: Data from different sources must be comparable and usable together.
- **Transparency**: The evaluation process must be transparent, ensuring that results can be replicated.

By adhering to these principles, organizations can demonstrate that their geospatial data meets the necessary quality standards for a range of applications.

1.2. Use of Accepted Sampling and Evaluation Methods

Conformance to the standard requires that organizations employ **appropriate sampling methods** and evaluation techniques, as outlined in **Clause 6** of the standard. The **sampling methods** should ensure that the evaluation results are **statistically valid** and **representative** of the entire dataset.

Organizations must use established methods such as:

- **Random sampling**: For general-purpose assessments.
- **Stratified sampling**: For datasets with distinct categories (e.g., different land use types).
- **Systematic sampling**: For spatially uniform datasets.

1.3. Comprehensive Reporting of Evaluation Results

Conformance to **ISO 19157:2023** also requires that organizations **report** their evaluation results following the guidelines in **Clause 7**. This includes providing detailed **metadata**, quantifiable results for each data quality element (e.g., **accuracy**, **completeness**), and **uncertainty levels** associated with the evaluation.

A **data quality evaluation report** should clearly present:

- **Evaluation objectives and criteria**

- **Sampling methods used**
- **Findings on data quality** (e.g., positional accuracy, completeness)
- **Uncertainty and limitations** in the data

1.4. Addressing Uncertainty and Limitations

To conform to **ISO 19157:2023**, organizations must recognize and report **uncertainty** and **limitations** in their data quality evaluation. This includes understanding and communicating the **error margins** in data measurements, the potential for **missing data**, and the inherent limitations in the evaluation process itself.

This transparency helps ensure that data users are aware of the **uncertainty** in the data and can interpret results with a full understanding of the data's limitations.

2. HOW TO DEMONSTRATE COMPLIANCE WITH ISO 19157:2023

Compliance with **ISO 19157:2023** can be demonstrated by following a structured process of **data evaluation**, reporting, and continual improvement. Here's how an organization can demonstrate **compliance** with the standard:

2.1. Implementing a Data Quality Management System (DQMS)

A **Data Quality Management System (DQMS)** provides the organizational framework to monitor and improve data quality continuously. The **DQMS** should:

- **Document procedures**: Outline the steps for data quality evaluation, including sampling, analysis, and reporting.
- **Set quality objectives**: Define specific quality targets (e.g., 95% positional accuracy).
- **Monitor data quality**: Regularly assess data quality against established standards and benchmarks.
- **Implement corrective actions**: If data quality does not meet the standards, develop action plans to correct deficiencies.

2.2. Establishing a Data Quality Certification Process

Organizations can **certify** that their data meets the **requirements** of **ISO 19157:2023** through independent **audits** or **third-party certifications**. The certification process typically involves:

- **Data evaluation** by a third-party auditor who applies the standards and evaluates the organization's data quality practices.
- **Certification** based on compliance with the standard's criteria, including the use of proper **sampling methods**, **reporting practices**, and **evaluation methods**.
- **Ongoing monitoring** to ensure that the organization continues to meet the certification requirements.

2.3. Training and Awareness Programs

For **ISO 19157:2023** compliance, organizations should ensure that their **staff** is trained in the principles of **data quality** and the **requirements** of the standard. Key aspects of training should include:

- **Data quality principles**: Ensuring staff understand the importance of **consistency**, **comparability**, and **transparency** in data evaluations.
- **Sampling techniques**: Educating employees on the **different sampling methods** and how to apply them correctly.
- **Reporting requirements**: Teaching staff how to document and report data quality evaluations in accordance with the standard.

2.4. Continuous Improvement and Feedback Loop

Compliance with **ISO 19157:2023** requires that organizations **continually improve** their data quality practices. This includes:

- **Regular data quality assessments** to identify areas for improvement.
- **Feedback mechanisms** that allow stakeholders to provide input on data quality.
- **Reevaluating data quality** periodically to adapt to new requirements, technologies, or business needs.

3. TABLE: CONFORMANCE AND COMPLIANCE EVALUATION CHECKLIST

Below is a sample table to help organizations assess their **conformance** and **compliance** with **ISO 19157:2023**:

Conformance/Compliance Aspect	Description	Evidence of Compliance
Data Quality Principles	Adherence to principles of **consistency**, **comparability**, and **transparency**.	Documentation of evaluation methods and criteria.
Sampling and Evaluation Methods	Use of valid **sampling methods** and consistent evaluation techniques.	Sampling plan and evaluation reports.
Reporting	Clear and comprehensive **data quality evaluation reports.**	Sample evaluation report, metadata documentation.
Uncertainty Reporting	Acknowledgement and reporting of **uncertainty** in evaluation results.	Report sections detailing uncertainty and limitations.
Data Quality Management System	Implementation of a **DQMS** to monitor and improve data quality.	Evidence of an active DQMS and regular assessments.
Training and Awareness	Ongoing **training programs** for staff on data quality principles and practices.	Records of training sessions and certifications.

SUMMARY

Conforming to **ISO 19157:2023** ensures that geospatial data meets **defined quality standards** and is fit for its intended purpose. By adhering to the **data quality principles**, using appropriate **sampling and evaluation methods**, and providing **clear and transparent reporting**, organizations can demonstrate their **compliance** with the standard. Additionally, a **Data Quality Management System (DQMS)**, along with **regular assessments** and **staff training**, ensures ongoing compliance and continual improvement in data quality practices.

HOW TO DEMONSTRATE CONFORMANCE WITH EVALUATION PROCEDURES AND DOCUMENTATION

Demonstrating **conformance** with **evaluation procedures** and **documentation** in line with **ISO 19157:2023** ensures that data quality assessments are performed consistently, transparently, and in a way that can be verified. This section outlines practical steps for **documenting data quality evaluations**, **ensuring compliance**, and maintaining **audit readiness** over time.

1. DOCUMENTATION OF EVALUATION PROCEDURES

1.1. Define Evaluation Procedures Clearly

- **Standardized Methodology**: Establish clear and standardized **data evaluation procedures** that align with **ISO 19157:2023**. This should include well-defined steps for:
    - **Data collection** (e.g., sampling techniques, tools used)
    - **Data validation** (e.g., automated checks, manual reviews)
    - **Data reporting** (e.g., evaluation results, uncertainty assessments).
- **Document Sampling Methods**: Ensure that **sampling techniques** used (e.g., random, stratified) are fully documented and align with the requirements for **statistical validity** and **representativeness**. This includes:
    - **Sample size** determination.
    - **Criteria** for selecting samples.
    - **Sampling frequency** (for continuous or periodic evaluations).

1.2. Maintain Comprehensive Metadata

- **Metadata Standards**: Use established **metadata standards** such as **ISO 19115** to document the **evaluation methods**, **data quality** criteria, and **sampling processes**. Metadata should also include:
    - **Sampling dates** and **evaluation periods**.
    - **Uncertainty measures** related to data quality.
    - **Software and tools** used for evaluation and reporting.
- **Metadata Storage**: Ensure metadata is stored in an accessible, structured format (e.g., database, document repository) that allows for easy retrieval during audits.

2. ESTABLISHING AND MAINTAINING COMPLIANCE WITH ISO 19157:2023

2.1. Set Up a Data Quality Management System (DQMS)

A **Data Quality Management System (DQMS)** helps manage the processes involved in ensuring compliance with **ISO 19157:2023**. A well-established **DQMS** should include:

- **Quality Standards**: Establish clear **data quality standards** (e.g., accuracy thresholds, acceptable error margins) that meet the requirements of **ISO 19157:2023**.
- **Procedural Guidelines**: Develop **detailed procedural guidelines** that define how data quality evaluations should be conducted, who is responsible for each step, and how results should be reported.
- **Regular Monitoring**: Set up a system for **continuous monitoring** and **re-evaluating** data quality against defined standards. This ensures ongoing compliance with ISO standards.

2.2. Implement Internal Audits and Reviews

- **Internal Audits**: Conduct **regular internal audits** of the data quality evaluation processes to assess conformance with **ISO 19157:2023**. These audits should:
    - Check that the **sampling methods** are correctly applied.
    - Validate that the **data evaluation** is based on **established criteria** and **standards**.
    - Review the **documentation** and **metadata** for accuracy and completeness.
- **Corrective Actions**: After each audit, ensure that any **non-conformances** identified are addressed through **corrective actions**. This could involve revising evaluation procedures, retraining staff, or improving data collection methods.

2.3. Use Version Control for Documents and Procedures

- **Version Control**: Implement a **version control system** (e.g., Git) for tracking changes to **evaluation procedures**, **documentation**, and **sampling methods**. This ensures that:
  - Previous versions of documents and procedures are retained for **audit purposes**.
  - Any updates to procedures are clearly documented and reviewed.
- **Documentation Updates**: Ensure that all changes to **evaluation procedures** or **data quality standards** are well-documented and communicated to relevant stakeholders. All updates should also be reflected in the metadata.

3. ENSURING LONG-TERM COMPLIANCE AND AUDIT READINESS

3.1. Continuous Training and Skill Development

- **Training Programs**: Establish **continuous training programs** for staff involved in data evaluation, ensuring they understand the **ISO 19157:2023** requirements and are skilled in **sampling**, **data evaluation**, and **reporting**.
  - Offer periodic refresher courses to keep staff updated on the latest standards and tools.
  - Provide **hands-on training** for tools used in data quality evaluation and reporting.
- **Certification**: Encourage certification for staff in **data quality management** and related standards to ensure they possess the necessary qualifications for conducting evaluations in accordance with **ISO 19157:2023**.

3.2. Regular Data Quality Assessments

- **Scheduled Reviews**: Set up a regular schedule for **data quality assessments** to ensure that data continuously meets the required standards. This should include both:
  - **Periodic reviews** of the dataset (e.g., quarterly, annually).
  - **Ad-hoc reviews** triggered by major updates or significant changes to the data.

- **Continuous Monitoring Tools**: Use **automated tools** to monitor data quality in real time and generate **alerts** when data quality falls below predefined thresholds.

3.3. Maintain Clear Reporting Procedures

- **Audit-Ready Reports**: Ensure that all data quality evaluations are documented in clear, concise **evaluation reports** that can be easily reviewed during internal or external audits. Reports should include:
    - **Summary of findings**: A clear summary of data quality evaluation results.
    - **Methodology**: Detailed descriptions of the **sampling methods**, **evaluation techniques**, and **tools** used.
    - **Recommendations for improvement**: Any actionable steps to improve data quality.
    - **Uncertainty**: Document **uncertainty levels** associated with the evaluation results.
- **Documentation Repository**: Store all evaluation reports, metadata, and related documentation in a centralized **document management system**. This ensures that the documentation is easily accessible for future audits or compliance checks.

4. PRACTICAL STEPS FOR MAINTAINING LONG-TERM COMPLIANCE AND AUDIT READINESS

4.1. Establish and Implement Data Quality Frameworks

- Develop a **comprehensive data quality framework** that aligns with **ISO 19157:2023** and provides **clear guidelines** on how data should be managed, evaluated, and reported over time.
- Integrate the framework into the organization's **data governance processes** to ensure long-term adherence to quality standards.

4.2. Monitor Regulatory Changes and Adapt

- **Track updates** to **ISO 19157:2023** and other relevant regulations to ensure compliance is always up-to-date.

- **Adjust procedures** accordingly if there are any changes in the standard or in industry best practices.

4.3. Set Up a Compliance Dashboard

- Use a **compliance dashboard** to track and visualize **data quality compliance metrics** in real-time. This tool can highlight areas where the organization is falling short and ensure that corrective actions are taken promptly.

SUMMARY

Demonstrating **conformance** with **ISO 19157:2023** requires clear **documentation**, adherence to **sampling and evaluation procedures**, and the establishment of a **data quality management system** that ensures continuous improvement. By implementing best practices for **training**, **auditing**, and **reporting**, organizations can maintain **long-term compliance** and **audit readiness**, ensuring that their data quality evaluation processes remain robust, transparent, and reliable.

CHAPTER 5

Implementing ISO 19157:2023 in Modern Data Systems

IMPLEMENTING ISO 19157:2023 IN MODERN DATA SYSTEMS

In today's world, **geospatial data** is increasingly being processed by **AI** and **automated systems** to generate insights and facilitate decision-making. The application of **ISO 19157:2023**, which defines standards for **data quality evaluation**, is crucial for ensuring that **automated systems** and **AI models** work with reliable, accurate, and complete geospatial data.

This chapter focuses on the integration of **ISO 19157:2023** into **AI-based** and **automated geospatial data workflows**, covering how to manage the **quality of data inputs** to **AI models** and how to ensure **compliance** with the standard in the context of modern data systems.

1. AI AND AUTOMATION IN DATA QUALITY EVALUATION

AI and automation are revolutionizing the way **geospatial data** is collected, processed, and analyzed. However, the effectiveness of AI and automated systems relies heavily on the quality of the data they process. **ISO 19157:2023** provides the framework necessary to ensure that data used in **AI systems** is **reliable**, **accurate**, and **fit for purpose**.

1.1. AI and Automation in Data Quality Assessment

AI and **machine learning** (ML) algorithms can be applied to automate various aspects of the **data quality evaluation** process. This includes:

- **Automated Data Cleaning**: AI tools can be used to detect and correct errors in geospatial datasets (e.g., removing **duplicate entries**, correcting **spatial inaccuracies**, and identifying **gaps** in the data).
- **Quality Monitoring**: AI algorithms can continuously monitor **data quality** by flagging instances where the data falls below predefined quality thresholds (e.g., **accuracy**, **completeness**). These systems can alert stakeholders when data quality is compromised.
- **Pattern Recognition**: Machine learning algorithms can automatically detect patterns or anomalies in large geospatial datasets, which helps identify **data inconsistencies** or issues with **data quality** (e.g., detecting **incorrect classifications** in land use data).
- **Data Validation**: AI models can be trained to validate data quality by comparing new datasets against **reference datasets** or **ground truth data**, ensuring consistency and accuracy.

Application of ISO 19157:2023 in AI-based and Automated Geospatial Workflows

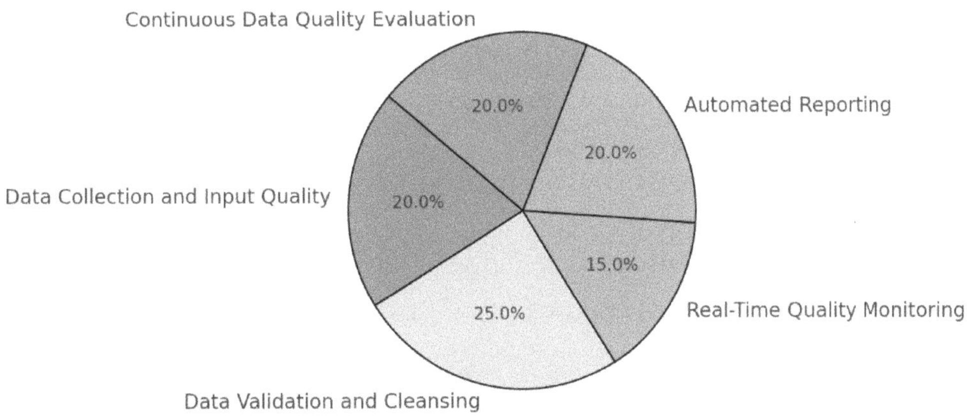

1.2. Benefits of AI and Automation in Data Quality Evaluation

- **Efficiency and Scalability**: AI can process vast amounts of geospatial data far more quickly than manual methods, making it possible to evaluate data quality at **scale**.
- **Real-Time Quality Monitoring**: Automated systems powered by AI can provide **real-time** data quality assessments, ensuring that data used in decision-making is always up-to-date and meets quality standards.

- **Consistency and Objectivity**: AI systems operate based on predefined criteria, ensuring consistent and **objective evaluations** of data quality without human bias.

2. APPLICATION OF ISO 19157:2023 IN AI-BASED AND AUTOMATED GEOSPATIAL DATA WORKFLOWS

Integrating **ISO 19157:2023** into AI-based and automated geospatial workflows ensures that data quality is maintained throughout the lifecycle of the data, from **collection** and **processing** to **analysis** and **reporting**.

2.1. Ensuring Data Quality in AI-Based Geospatial Data Workflows

For AI systems to make **accurate predictions** or provide **insights**, the data they are trained on must meet high standards of **quality**. **ISO 19157:2023** provides a structured approach to ensuring that this data meets the required quality levels.

Key Steps in Implementing ISO 19157:2023 in AI Workflows:

1. **Data Collection and Input Quality**:
   - Ensure that data collected for training AI models meets **quality standards** from the outset.
   - **ISO 19157:2023** outlines methods for ensuring **completeness**, **accuracy**, and **consistency** in the collected data.
2. **Data Validation**:
   - **Automated validation** checks should be implemented to verify that data input into AI models meets predefined **data quality standards**.
   - **AI-based validation tools** can compare new data against **reference datasets** to assess its **positional accuracy**, **completeness**, and **logical consistency**.
3. **Real-Time Data Quality Evaluation**:
   - Use **AI systems** to **continuously evaluate** data quality during the analysis phase, ensuring that any issues are identified and addressed quickly.
   - For instance, when using **geospatial data** for mapping, AI can check that features like roads or boundaries are properly aligned and complete.
4. **Model Training and Validation**:

- **ISO 19157:2023** emphasizes the need for **reliable training data**. Ensuring that the datasets used to train AI models are of high quality is critical to improving the **performance** and **accuracy** of these models.
- Implement **automated workflows** to assess and improve the quality of **training data** before it is fed into AI algorithms.

2.2. Automation of Data Quality Evaluation

Automation plays a key role in maintaining high data quality standards throughout the data lifecycle. By applying **ISO 19157:2023**, organizations can ensure that **automated systems** follow standardized procedures to maintain quality.

Key Areas for Automation in Geospatial Workflows:

- **Automated Sampling and Evaluation**: Automated systems can implement **sampling methods** defined in **ISO 19157:2023** (e.g., random or stratified sampling) to evaluate the quality of datasets in an ongoing fashion.
- **Automated Reporting**: Use **AI-driven reporting tools** to automatically generate **data quality reports** that adhere to the standards outlined in **Clause** 7 of ISO 19157:2023. These reports can provide insights on the **accuracy**, **completeness**, and **consistency** of datasets used in AI systems.
- **Continuous Monitoring**: Implement systems that use **AI algorithms** to continuously monitor the **quality** of incoming geospatial data, flagging issues related to **accuracy** or **completeness** as they arise.

3. MANAGING THE QUALITY OF DATA INPUTS TO AI MODELS AND ENSURING COMPLIANCE

Ensuring that **AI models** are fed with **high-quality data** is essential for producing accurate results. By maintaining compliance with **ISO 19157:2023**, organizations can ensure that data inputs meet the necessary standards for quality, reliability, and compliance.

3.1. Managing Input Data Quality for AI Models

To ensure that **AI models** work effectively, **data quality** must be actively managed at the input stage:

- **Data Cleansing**: Implement **automated data cleansing** procedures that align with **ISO 19157:2023** to remove inconsistencies, duplicates, and errors from geospatial datasets before they are used as input to AI models.
- **Data Transformation**: Standardize the format of input data, ensuring that all geospatial data conforms to consistent standards (e.g., coordinate systems, units of measurement), as outlined in **ISO 19157:2023**.
- **Data Quality Control**: Implement **quality control** checks to ensure that data used to train AI models meets predefined thresholds for **accuracy**, **completeness**, and **consistency**.

3.2. Ensuring Compliance in AI-Based Workflows

Ensuring that AI workflows comply with **ISO 19157:2023** involves:

- **Compliance Audits**: Regularly audit AI workflows to ensure that data quality checks align with the requirements of the standard. This includes evaluating the **sampling methods** used, **validation techniques**, and **reporting** of data quality results.
- **Data Quality Dashboards**: Use **real-time dashboards** to track and visualize data quality metrics, ensuring that data inputs into AI models meet compliance standards at all stages of processing.
- **Automated Compliance Monitoring**: Implement **AI-driven compliance monitoring** tools that continuously check whether the input data to AI models conforms to **ISO 19157:2023** standards.

SUMMARY

Implementing **ISO 19157:2023** in **AI-based** and **automated geospatial data workflows** ensures that **data quality** is maintained across the entire lifecycle. By integrating **automated data quality evaluation**, **real-time monitoring**, and **continuous training of AI models**, organizations can ensure that the data fed into AI systems is accurate, complete, and reliable. This adherence to **ISO 19157:2023** standards supports **compliance**, improves **decision-making**, and enhances the **accuracy** of AI-driven insights in geospatial data systems.

ALIGNING ORGANIZATIONAL DATA SYSTEMS WITH ISO 19157:2023

Integrating **ISO 19157:2023** into **data management workflows** helps organizations ensure that their **geospatial data** is of high quality, enabling **better decision-making**, **efficiency**, and **compliance** with international standards. This process involves aligning existing data management systems with the **data quality principles** and guidelines defined in the standard.

This section outlines **how to integrate ISO 19157:2023** into your existing data systems and provides **case studies** of organizations that have successfully aligned their systems with the standard.

1. UNDERSTANDING ISO 19157:2023

ISO 19157:2023 sets out guidelines for evaluating **geospatial data quality**. This includes assessing aspects such as:

- **Completeness** (whether all necessary data is present).
- **Consistency** (data should conform to predefined rules).
- **Accuracy** (data should correctly represent real-world features).
- **Positional accuracy** (spatial correctness of geospatial data).
- **Temporal accuracy** (accuracy related to time references in the data).

To successfully integrate **ISO 19157:2023**, your organization must align its **data management processes** with these core principles.

2. HOW TO INTEGRATE ISO 19157:2023 INTO YOUR EXISTING DATA MANAGEMENT WORKFLOWS

Integrating **ISO 19157:2023** involves making changes to data collection, evaluation, and reporting procedures within your existing systems. Here are the steps involved:

2.1. Establish Data Quality Standards and Objectives

- **Define Data Quality Goals**: Align your organization's data quality objectives with the **core principles** of **ISO 19157:2023**. Set measurable targets for key quality elements, such as **accuracy**, **completeness**, and **usability**.

- **Incorporate ISO 19157:2023 Criteria**: Update internal standards and documentation to include data quality evaluation criteria from **ISO 19157:2023**. These should be used to assess new and existing datasets regularly.

2.2. Standardize Data Collection Procedures

- **Align Data Collection Methods**: Ensure that data collection methods align with the standards specified in **ISO 19157:2023**. This includes ensuring **spatial accuracy** and **completeness** when collecting geospatial data.
- **Sampling Techniques**: Implement sampling methods like **random sampling**, **stratified sampling**, and **systematic sampling** to evaluate the quality of geospatial data. This can be automated in systems to ensure compliance at scale.
- **Data Entry Protocols**: Standardize **data input protocols** to ensure data entered into the system adheres to **ISO 19157:2023** criteria, especially in terms of accuracy, consistency, and completeness.

2.3. Implement Automated Data Quality Evaluation

- **Automated Quality Checks**: Use **automated systems** for real-time data quality evaluation. This can include:
    - **Automated validation checks** to assess completeness and accuracy.
    - **Consistency checks** to ensure data conforms to expected rules and formats.
- **AI for Quality Monitoring**: Implement **AI-driven systems** to continuously monitor data quality, identify anomalies, and flag errors as they arise, ensuring that data is always in conformance with quality standards.

2.4. Integrate Data Quality Reporting Systems

- **Automated Reporting**: Develop **automated reporting systems** that generate **data quality reports** based on **ISO 19157:2023** criteria. These reports should include:
    - Evaluation of key quality elements such as **accuracy**, **completeness**, and **logical consistency**.
    - Identification of any data issues, such as **missing data** or **inconsistent data entries**.

- **Dashboards for Monitoring**: Implement **real-time dashboards** to track data quality metrics and enable stakeholders to visualize the health of the data at any time.

2.5. Maintain Comprehensive Metadata

- **Document Metadata**: Ensure that **metadata** is documented for all datasets in accordance with **ISO 19115**, which is referenced by **ISO 19157:2023**. Metadata should include:
    - **Data collection methods** and **sampling procedures**.
    - **Data quality evaluation results** and **uncertainty levels**.
- **Centralized Metadata Storage**: Store metadata in a **centralized system** that is accessible for audits and compliance checks, ensuring transparency and traceability.

2.6. Continuous Training and Awareness

- **Staff Training**: Train staff regularly on the principles of **ISO 19157:2023** and the importance of **data quality**. Ensure that they understand:
    - How to collect and evaluate data based on **ISO standards**.
    - How to use automated systems and tools to assess data quality.
- **Create Awareness**: Foster an organizational culture of **data quality awareness**, ensuring all employees understand their role in maintaining high-quality geospatial data.

3. CASE STUDIES OF ORGANIZATIONS SUCCESSFULLY ALIGNING WITH ISO 19157:2023

Here are a few examples of organizations that successfully integrated **ISO 19157:2023** into their existing data management workflows:

3.1. Case Study: A National Mapping Agency

A **national mapping agency** responsible for creating and maintaining **topographic maps** and **spatial data** for a country implemented **ISO 19157:2023** to enhance the quality and consistency of its geospatial datasets.

Steps Taken:

- The agency established clear **data quality objectives** aligned with **ISO 19157:2023** standards.
- Automated systems were put in place to evaluate **positional accuracy** and **completeness** of new data collected from **satellite imagery** and **field surveys**.
- **Metadata standards** were updated to include **ISO 19157:2023** criteria, ensuring that all data collections were documented with quality metrics.

Outcome:

- The agency saw an improvement in the **accuracy** and **reliability** of its national datasets, which are used by various governmental departments and the public for decision-making and planning.

3.2. Case Study: Environmental Monitoring Organization

An **environmental monitoring organization** responsible for collecting geospatial data on air quality, water quality, and deforestation integrated **ISO 19157:2023** to ensure that its **sensor networks** and **survey data** met high standards for **data quality**.

Steps Taken:

- The organization developed a **Data Quality Management System (DQMS)** to continuously monitor the **quality** of incoming sensor data.
- Automated **real-time quality checks** were applied to detect data **gaps** or **inconsistencies** in air and water quality measurements.
- **Uncertainty** related to data from various sensors was documented in the **metadata** for transparency.

Outcome:

- The integration of **ISO 19157:2023** improved the **accuracy** of environmental reports and ensured **data reliability**, making it easier for stakeholders to make **informed environmental decisions**.

3.3. Case Study: Smart City Initiative

A city government undertaking a **smart city initiative** integrated **ISO 19157:2023** to improve the quality of **geospatial data** used for **urban planning**, **traffic management**, and **public services**.

Steps Taken:

- The city set up a **centralized data management platform** that adhered to **ISO 19157:2023** standards, ensuring that all geospatial data used for planning and services was consistently evaluated for **completeness**, **accuracy**, and **logical consistency**.
- **AI-driven tools** were deployed to analyze traffic patterns and **predictive models** for urban development.

Outcome:

- The integration led to better **resource allocation**, improved **traffic management**, and more **sustainable urban planning** practices, all based on high-quality geospatial data.

4. PRACTICAL STEPS FOR ORGANIZATIONS TO ALIGN WITH ISO 19157:2023

Step	Action	Outcome
Define Data Quality Objectives	Align organizational data quality objectives with **ISO 19157:2023** principles.	Clear data quality goals and measurable targets.
Standardize Data Collection	Implement standardized data collection methods that align with **ISO 19157:2023**.	Consistent, high-quality data collection across all systems.
Automate Quality Evaluation	Implement automated systems for real-time data quality evaluation.	Timely detection of data quality issues and automatic remediation.
Update Metadata Practices	Document metadata in accordance with **ISO 19115** and **ISO 19157:2023**.	Transparent and accessible metadata supporting data traceability.

Train Staff	Provide ongoing training to staff on **ISO 19157:2023** data quality standards.	A well-informed team capable of managing and evaluating data quality.
Continuous Monitoring	Establish automated monitoring for continuous data quality assurance.	Ongoing assurance of data quality compliance.

SUMMARY

Aligning your organization's **data management workflows** with **ISO 19157:2023** ensures that **geospatial data** meets high-quality standards, allowing for better decision-making, operational efficiency, and compliance. By implementing **automated evaluation tools**, **standardizing data collection**, and **integrating real-time monitoring**, organizations can maintain long-term compliance with **ISO 19157:2023**. Case studies of successful implementations show how the standard can enhance the **accuracy**, **consistency**, and **usability** of data across a range of industries, from **government agencies** to **smart cities**.

SUSTAINING DATA QUALITY IN CHANGING ENVIRONMENTS

In an era of rapid technological advancement, maintaining **data quality** and ensuring ongoing **conformance** with standards like **ISO 19157:2023** is essential for organizations to stay agile and responsive. As data collection methods and technologies evolve, organizations must remain proactive in ensuring their data systems remain compliant and adaptable to changes.

This chapter outlines how to sustain **data quality** and **conformance** with **ISO 19157:2023** in a constantly changing landscape. It provides practical strategies for preparing for future revisions of the standard and maintaining **adaptability** in data governance practices.

1. ENSURING ONGOING CONFORMANCE AS TECHNOLOGY AND DATA COLLECTION METHODS EVOLVE

As technology and data collection methods evolve, it's crucial that organizations maintain **data quality** while ensuring that their practices align with **ISO 19157:2023**. Here's how organizations can ensure **ongoing conformance** to the standard:

1.1. Embrace Automation and AI in Data Collection and Evaluation

- **Automate Data Collection and Monitoring**: As technologies like **IoT** and **AI** become increasingly prevalent, data collection methods evolve. Ensure your systems are capable of integrating **automated data validation**, **AI-driven analysis**, and **real-time monitoring** tools that align with **ISO 19157:2023**.
  - Use **AI-based tools** to continuously check the **quality** of incoming data and flag issues as they arise.
  - Implement **machine learning** models that can automatically identify anomalies in **geospatial data** and assess **accuracy** in real time.
- **Adapt Data Collection Tools**: As new data collection technologies, such as **drones**, **satellite sensors**, or **GPS devices**, evolve, ensure that your systems are adaptable and can **easily integrate new sources of data** while maintaining consistent **data quality standards**.

1.2. Implement Flexible Data Quality Frameworks

- **Develop Flexible Quality Assurance Frameworks**: Create **data quality frameworks** that can be easily adapted to new technologies and methodologies. These frameworks should include:
  - **Modular quality checks** that can be applied to different types of data or new data sources.
  - **Regular updates** to data quality evaluation criteria to match advancements in **data collection technologies**.
- **Ongoing Reviews**: Regularly review and update the data quality evaluation processes to ensure they are still aligned with **ISO 19157:2023**, especially as technology and methods change. This review process should include:
  - **Assessment of new data sources** (e.g., IoT, crowdsourced data) and their impact on data quality.
  - Integration of **new data standards** as they emerge in the industry or through future revisions of **ISO 19157**.

1.3. Leverage Real-Time Data Validation and Monitoring

- **Continuous Monitoring Systems**: Implement **real-time data validation** and **monitoring systems** that automatically assess data quality across different systems and processes.
    - Use **cloud-based tools** that provide **instant validation** of new data before it enters the system, ensuring that it meets **ISO 19157** criteria.
    - Establish **continuous feedback loops** for data quality, allowing for immediate action when issues are detected.
- **Performance Dashboards**: Create **real-time dashboards** to monitor the health of data quality and ensure that data quality stays consistent across different systems, regardless of evolving data collection methods or technologies.

2. PREPARING FOR FUTURE REVISIONS OF ISO 19157 AND MAINTAINING ADAPTABILITY IN DATA GOVERNANCE PRACTICES

As **ISO 19157** evolves and new versions of the standard are released, organizations must ensure they are prepared for these updates while maintaining **adaptability** in their **data governance practices**.

2.1. Establish a Data Governance Framework for Adaptability

- **Flexible Governance Models**: Develop a **data governance model** that is flexible enough to accommodate future changes in **data collection technologies, evaluation methods**, and **ISO revisions**.
    - Regularly update the **data governance framework** to align with new **data quality standards** and evolving industry best practices.
    - Ensure your governance practices allow for easy integration of **new data sources** and methodologies as technology advances.
- **Data Quality Leadership**: Establish a **dedicated data quality leadership team** that is responsible for staying current with revisions of **ISO 19157** and other relevant standards. This team should ensure that the organization adapts its **data quality policies** as needed.

2.2. Stay Ahead of Technological Advancements

- **Technology Scouting**: Regularly **scout for emerging technologies** in **data collection** (e.g., **5G networks**, **edge computing**, **satellite advancements**) and **data quality assurance** (e.g., **AI validation tools**, **blockchain for data provenance**) that could affect your data quality practices and **ISO 19157** compliance.
- **R&D Investment**: Invest in **research and development (R&D)** to explore how new technologies can be integrated into your data systems while maintaining **data quality**. This could include experimenting with **new sensors**, **machine learning models**, or **cloud-based data storage solutions**.

2.3. Maintain Regular Compliance Reviews and Audits

- **Regular Audits**: Perform **regular audits** of your data systems to ensure ongoing **compliance** with the latest version of **ISO 19157**. These audits should evaluate:
  - How well current data practices align with the latest **data quality principles**.
  - Whether new data sources or technologies have been adequately integrated into the data evaluation and management processes.
- **Feedback Loops for Improvement**: Use audit findings to implement improvements in **data collection**, **evaluation procedures**, and **reporting** processes to ensure the organization remains compliant and adaptable to changes in data quality standards.

2.4. Engage with ISO Committees and Industry Groups

- **Stay Informed**: Join **ISO committees** or **industry groups** that focus on **data quality standards** to stay informed about upcoming revisions to **ISO 19157** and other relevant standards.
- **Participate in Public Consultation**: When **ISO 19157** revisions are proposed, participate in public consultations or provide feedback to help shape future versions of the standard.

3. PRACTICAL STEPS FOR SUSTAINING DATA QUALITY IN CHANGING ENVIRONMENTS

Step	Action	Outcome
Develop Flexible Data Governance	Design governance frameworks that adapt to new data sources and technologies.	Agile data governance that can evolve with technology.
Continuous Monitoring and Auditing	Implement automated data quality monitoring and regular audits.	Real-time monitoring of data quality across systems.
Invest in Technology Scouting	Regularly review emerging technologies and innovations in data collection.	Early adoption of technologies that support data quality.
Training and Skill Development	Provide ongoing training on ISO standards and new technologies.	Well-prepared team with the skills to handle evolving standards.
Maintain Regular Compliance Reviews	Perform regular internal audits to ensure compliance with ISO 19157:2023.	Ongoing alignment with ISO standards and best practices.
Adapt Data Quality Frameworks	Review and adapt data quality frameworks to accommodate new data types.	Flexibility in data systems to handle evolving data and tech needs.

SUMMARY

Sustaining **data quality** in **changing environments** requires proactive planning and adaptability. By embracing **automated systems**, fostering **flexible data governance**, and staying **ahead of technological advancements**, organizations can ensure that their data remains **high-quality**, **compliant**, and **fit for purpose**, even as **ISO 19157:2023** evolves over time. Through continuous **monitoring**, **audit processes**, and **training**, organizations can maintain **data quality** and ensure they are prepared for future updates to the standard, thereby enhancing their long-term **data governance practices** and supporting **reliable decision-making**.

Thank you for exploring the essentials of **ISO 19157:2023** and its application to **data quality management**. As data continues to drive decision-making in organizations worldwide, it's more critical than ever to ensure that your data systems remain **reliable**, **accurate**, and **compliant** with established standards.

By integrating the principles of **ISO 19157** into your **data management workflows**, adopting **automated quality assurance**, and fostering an organizational culture focused on **data quality**, your organization will be well-equipped to navigate the evolving landscape of **geospatial data**.

Remember, maintaining **data quality** is a continuous journey, one that requires ongoing adaptation to **new technologies**, evolving standards, and emerging data collection methods. **ISO 19157:2023** provides the framework for ensuring that your data not only meets today's needs but is also ready for the future.

Thank you for taking this step toward mastering data quality. We encourage you to stay engaged, adapt to changes, and continue prioritizing the integrity of your data.

www.ingramcontent.com/pod-product-compliance
Lightning Source LLC
Chambersburg PA
CBHW041748220926
51847CB00013B/143
* 9 7 8 3 8 5 2 2 8 1 2 7 8 *